People Make the Difference

People Make the Difference

Prescriptions and Profiles
of High Performance

by

Timothy J. Herron
George P. Bohan
Robert P. Meyer

with Florence Mustric

© 1997

published for

WINOC
Work In Northeast Ohio Council

by

Oakhill Press • Akron & New York

People Make the Difference

Library of Congress Cataloging-in-Publication Data

People Make the Difference
        232 pp.   cm.
    ISBN 1-886939-15-2
    1. Management--Ohio--Cleveland Metropolitan Area--Case
    studies. 2. Work environment--Ohio--Cleveland Metropolitan
    Area--Case studies.
    HD70.U52C637   1996
    659--dc21   96-44036
                                                        CIP

0 9 8 7 6 5 4 3 2 1

First Printing, December 1996

Recently I had the pleasure, along with some other business and civic leaders from Cleveland, of attending "Cleveland Day at Harvard Business School." I can't tell you how good it felt to bask in the limelight shining on the Turnaround City and to realize how far our business community has come in the past 15 years.

I remember how Rand Corporation evaluated and ranked America's top 105 cities for their potential to grow and remain competitive. When they did that survey in the late 1970s, they ranked Cleveland as 103 of 105.

In 1980 McKinsey & Company issued a study for Cleveland Tomorrow, a local group of CEOs, that said our manufacturing companies would continue to be important for Greater Cleveland's future, and that we had to help them become more competitive as quickly as possible. That led to the creation of a number of service organizations designed specifically to help bring about such changes. One of them is WINOC, the Work In Northeast Ohio Council. Our focus was designed to assist with innovations through people—through concepts and methods involved in customer-focused improvement, mutual trust, empowerment, an environment of continuous learning, and creative compensation systems—all part of what we refer to in this book as high-performance work practices.

The McKinsey study also showed that many companies decided not to relocate or expand to our region because of our historic labor-management problems. Accordingly, we have been helping labor and management work together to produce successes for business and in turn to make the community more competitive.

A number of other organizations also are working to help companies become more successful. These organizations include universities, community colleges, and technical schools; chambers of commerce; and a number of private and nonprofit organizations.

We have leveraged our efforts by working with partners such as the Greater Cleveland Growth Association's Council of Smaller Enterprises, to reach small business; Cleveland Advanced Manufacturing Program, for innovations through technology; and educational institutions, for teaching basic skills.

Today it is well-documented that high-performance work practices produce tangible and significant results. For example, in the Summer 1996 issue of *Organizational Dynamics*, Jeffrey Pfeffer enumerates results in a variety of industries. His examples include: 47% better quality using flexible manufacturing techniques instead of mass-production methods; 80% less downtime using high-commitment work practices instead of control-oriented management; and 22% higher growth in gross margins over a four-year period in companies using team-based work and compensation systems.

In this book we profile some of Northeast Ohio's high-performance companies. These organizations provide proof that high-performance work systems can turn decline or failure into success, and success into even greater success. These companies are testimony to Greater Cleveland's comeback and to the continuing importance of manufacturing to our region.

Having worked with many companies over the past 15 years, we have seen what works when companies seek to implement high-performance work practices. We have also seen barriers that make the process needlessly difficult. We have written this book to document the experience and insight we have gained from assisting more than 500 organizations with their efforts to implement these practices.

In the *Prescriptions* section of this book, we describe how to involve people—the most underutilized resource in many organizations—and we demonstrate how people can make the difference in any organization's pursuit of high performance.

Your company and its people have what it takes. We wish you every success!

Robert P. Meyer
President, WINOC

ACKNOWLEDGMENTS

Many people have helped to make this book a reality.

The principal author was Tim Herron, Vice President of WINOC, with assistance from George Bohan and Robert Meyer. We thank East Ohio Gas Company for permission to use George Bohan's case study as the basis of our Profile of Ford Engine Plant 2.

The *Prescriptions* section of this book draws extensively from the articles written over the years by WINOC advisors, especially George Bohan, Jim Burton, Lynn Dupuy, Bob Gudgel, Tim Herron, Aubrey Mendelow, Marv Pozdol, and Jim Stephan.

Special thanks go to Florence Mustric, who wrote the *Profiles* and who helped edit and develop the insights of our advisors into a clear and thought-provoking book.

The idea for the book came from Carol Rivchun, our trusted Marketing Advisor, who insisted that after 15 years it was time to share the wisdom gleaned from our experiences, to document outstanding successes here in Northeast Ohio, and to encourage companies to continue their pursuit of high performance.

We also recognize the sponsors of this book, who saw the value of a resource document rooted in regional experiences. We thank BFGoodrich Company, LTV Steel Corporation, Oglebay Norton Company, Picker International, Pioneer-Standard Electronics, Inc., University Hospitals of Cleveland, and Van Dorn Demag Corporation.

We appreciate the ongoing support and encouragement of The Cleveland Foundation, The George Gund Foundation, and the Ohio Department of Development's Office of Labor and Management Cooperation.

DEDICATION

We dedicate this book to our chairman, Renold Thompson, and to our past chairmen, William B. Sellers, Jr., Ralph D. Ketchum, and Adolph Posnick, for their leadership in carrying out the mission of WINOC, namely to improve the economic climate and competitive position of businesses in Northeast Ohio and beyond by focusing on quality and productivity improvement through people.

TABLE OF CONTENTS

I. Prescriptions

DESIRE TO SURVIVE AND THRIVE

TABLE OF CONTENTS (CONTINUED)

High Performance

II. Profiles

Does your company achieve total customer satisfaction? Does everyone in the company share that vision and work to make it a reality? The trick is to translate the vision and everyone's energy into daily action—what you and others in your company actually need to do. How *do* you get to the next level of performance, and what does success actually look like?

Bringing this about will require new ways of doing things. These new ways are what we refer to as high-performance work systems. The companies that have used these systems and have achieved successful results are what we refer to as high-performance organizations.

Why we wrote this book

We had three reasons for writing this book. First, we realize that it's not easy to imagine what high-performance concepts will look like in practice. Even the people who are successfully employing them in their companies often have a hard time describing how everything fits together.

We also know that once you have a vision for the future of your company, the next challenge is to create a plan for how to get there. If you have a vision to be on a yacht in the South Pacific, you know that getting there will require some major changes. Creating a high-performance organization will also require major changes. If you continue to do the same things you did last week and last year, you're going to get essentially the same results. High performance is about getting very different results.

Second, we realize that most of the volumes that have been written on the subject (which may be referred to as total quality management, continuous quality improvement, or any of a variety of other names) deal with the big picture. They give an aerial photograph of the forest. A few of the books deal with the details of one small part of the process. They give a closeup view of a twig on one tree. Almost none deal with something vital in between—the tree; the major issues that involve the implementation of the concepts in your company. This is our focus.

Third, we have repeatedly found companies whose efforts have reached a plateau or have been derailed. These setbacks can be avoided. In this book we include strategies that will maximize your success with implementation.

Drawing on experience and insights

This book includes insights and lessons that we have learned and shared with hundreds of companies. As an organization, we have 15 years of experience to draw upon; individually, some of us have been involved with implementing these concepts for 25 years or more. We have a former Baldridge examiner, certified quality engineers, and certified ISO 9000 assessors. Our academic credentials include MBAs, masters in organizational development, and three doctorates. One member of our staff has 40 years of experience as a union leader. Our experience spans such functions as quality assurance, training, operations, labor relations, human resources, and hospital administration.

We have distilled this experience into an implementation guide on two levels. The first half of this book, which we call *Prescriptions*, walks through the essential elements of a time-tested implementation process. The second half, which we call *Profiles*, presents outstanding companies in Northeast Ohio and describes how they have achieved their successful performance levels.

Profiles of successful companies

People like to read about people, so we expect most readers to turn first to the *Profiles*. Here we set out to answer a number of questions: What do real people in real companies do to improve performance? What kinds of results do they get? What's most important? What's most difficult? What can other companies learn and apply?

Think of these *Profiles* as a series of benchmarking visits, with the emphasis not on the results but on the process used to achieve them. In a few of these profiles, we give a fairly comprehensive account of how the company went about involving its people in the creation of real performance improvement. In other cases, we focus on one or more aspects that we find to be outstanding and informative. These *Profiles* will be very helpful, particularly if you are in the early stages of implementation.

We focus on companies big and small, companies young and old, companies where the lights had been turned off, and successful companies looking for more growth. Most are manufacturers, but we also include distribution, service, and health-care organizations.

Most books highlight large national firms. We have focused on Northeast Ohio, but all these companies can hold their own in the national and the international marketplaces. Being local, they offer good opportunities for benchmarking.

These companies tackled implementation in slightly different ways, but all of them have discovered that the involvement of their people is what made the difference, and all of them have achieved high levels of performance.

You may find some that are comparable to your business, and you may be surprised that a very different type of business can offer useful insights and may even suggest a valuable paradigm shift, enabling you to look at your company or your industry in a totally different way.

Prescriptions for successful change

The other half of the book covers what we feel are the most important issues of the implementation process: our *Prescriptions* for change. In fact, the Table of Contents is a quick summary of the process we recommend. When we speak of implementation, we mean putting such a process into practice—a strategy that focuses on customer satisfaction, employee well-being and satisfaction, and positive operational and financial performance.

We have included things to remember, pitfalls to beware of, and some steps to follow. We describe how to do what needs to be done, why, and how it will help. We do *not*, however, describe it step-by-step. Compare this to a book on building houses, one that tells you how houses are built, what different types look like, and what to expect when you work with a builder to design and construct your own home.

Time and again experts say things like, "The key to making this work is that senior management has to be committed." To what? How? Even successful CEOs find it hard to describe their commitment in specific terms. We discuss what it should look like, what successful real-world leaders are committed *to*, and how that commitment came to be.

An interrelated never-ending cycle

It's to your advantage to begin by gaining a good understanding of what will be required to implement the entire process successfully. As you will see, we suggest starting with an assessment of your organization. On reaching the point where improvement initiatives are yielding results, you will have returned to the beginning of a never-ending cycle (after all, it *is* called continuous improvement). At that point you should assess the new situation and plan for further change.

When you are involved in implementing a specific activity, return to that chapter for a reminder of what you need to do and why. Use this book as a reference to evaluate your performance improvement plans and activities and to stay on track.

It's a whole new ball game

Keep in mind that continuous improvement and employee commitment to a company's vision of high performance will require a change in culture, and that your company's culture is rooted in generations of American companies and individuals doing things in a certain way.

This change in culture involves more than abstract concepts. It will require real people working together, continually searching for creative new ways to better serve other real people—your customers.

If high-performance work practices are to become a way of life, change *is* needed. Think. Plan. Above all, get started. You can read a book about how to play golf, but if you want to get good at the game, you have to go outside and start hitting balls. We hope this book will help you to get started or to continue on your journey, to surmount obstacles, and to reap the benefits of continuous improvement and high performance.

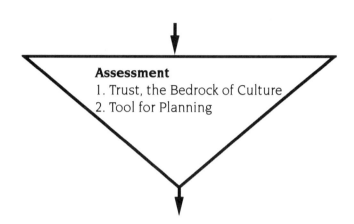

Assessment
1. Trust, the Bedrock of Culture
2. Tool for Planning

Before beginning any major organizational change, an assessment should be conducted to evaluate the current state of the organization's major systems, its culture, and the readiness of its people for change. The assessment serves to identify strengths and weaknesses, establishes a baseline measurement, provides objective data to be used in the planning process, and predicts barriers that will need to be overcome.

When an organization sets out to create a high-performance work system, that organization is embarking on a process that will transform its culture. The commitment to become a high-performance organization carries with it a commitment to certain cultural values, namely trust, communications, cooperation, empowerment, and innovation.

One of these values is of paramount importance: *trust*. Trust is the bedrock upon which the entire high-performance system and its supporting culture will be built. A high degree of trust between management and employees is absolutely essential in order to change the corporate culture and to create a truly high-performing organization.

Of the other four cultural values, effective communication helps to build trust. Cooperation, empowerment, and innovation are outcomes or byproducts of trust.

Build the culture on a bedrock of trust

Leadership must come to grips with the issue of trust up front. It won't be easy, but without trust an organization will never get the kinds of ideas that will result in significant improvements. Trust must be assessed directly at the beginning.

If sufficient trust does not exist, it's imperative to address and resolve the issue before proceeding with any other aspect of high performance. How does a company know if sufficient trust exists? An outside evaluation is usually necessary because leadership is too close to see the situation objectively.

The imperative of trust

In undertaking such extensive organizational change, where people are asked to continuously look at how the work is performed in order to make significant improvements, people need to know that their efforts won't backfire. If there is a culture of mistrust, people will look for a hidden agenda.

We know of no organization that has been truly successful in its change efforts without directly addressing the issue of job security. Management needs to make some kind of commitment that no employee will be laid off if improvements should reduce the need for people.

It's impossible to guarantee that the level of business will never decline. Likewise, it's unreasonable to expect a promise that layoffs will never occur (although some companies have done it). It *is* quite reasonable, however, to promise that any need for reduction in the workforce will be done by attrition. It *is* reasonable to promise that any people whose jobs are eliminated because of improvements may be moved to other jobs but won't be moved out the door.

In many organizations, there is an unwillingness to make these promises because of a hunger for the lesser short-term gains and the impatience to wait for the greater long-term gains. The usual result is that employees participate reluctantly or half-heartedly in improvement activities, which in turn yields minimal results in both the short and the long term.

How to build trust

Trust is based upon the ability to anticipate and to rely upon the actions of others, and the ability to understand and to rely upon what they say. Trust is built on common ground. A classic device used in illustrating how this works is the Johari Window:

	Known to Me	Unknown to Me
Known to Others	**Common Ground**	**Blind Area**
Unknown to Others	**Hidden Area**	**Unknown Potential**

Originators: Joseph Luft and Harry Ingham

When people share very little common ground, the Johari Window looks as follows:

	Known to Me	**Unknown to Me**
Known to Others	**Common Ground**	**Blind Area**
Unknown to Others	**Hidden Area**	**Unknown Potential**

Originators: Joseph Luft and Harry Ingham

This depicts a situation such as entering a room full of strangers. It also describes how management and employees interact in many traditional organizations, where there is very little trust.

In building trust, the goal is to increase the area of common ground so that the Johari Window looks more like this:

	Known to Me	**Unknown to Me**
Known to Others	**Common Ground**	**Blind Area**
Unknown to Others	**Hidden Area**	**Unknown Potential**

Originators: Joseph Luft and Harry Ingham

This is done via feedback (receiving information from others about one's behavior) and by self-disclosure (telling others more about oneself). These two actions will result in better communications among people at all levels and will enable them to build trust. As the common ground expands:

1. The gap decreases between the intent and the effect of communications;
2. Misperceptions are minimized, and people are seen by others as more truthful and credible; and
3. Trust is the natural consequence.

The need for common ground

Out of many possible illustrations, we think the following one vividly illustrates how insufficient common ground can create a gap between the intent and the effect of communications.

At one of our client companies, it became apparent that the president needed to demonstrate his support of teams and his interest in their work. So he went out onto the shop floor and asked questions of several team members about their team activity.

Instead of being seen as supportive, his actions resulted in total upheaval! Employees perceived his questions as criticism of their efforts. "How," employees asked, "can he be so suspicious of what we're doing when he's the one who asked us to do this in the first place?" Because the president had seldom communicated directly with the people on the teams, there was very little common ground between them, and consequently very little trust.

The solution was obvious. Before he could begin to demonstrate support, he had to build a sufficient level of trust between himself and the team members. To do that, he had to communicate directly with them much more frequently, both formally and informally.

Trust takes time to develop

How long will it take to establish trust? For the answer, look at how long it has taken for the lack of trust to build up. Old experiences and behaviors won't be abandoned overnight. And even with success and experience over time, things can happen that cause behavior to regress, and trust along with it. It will take time, serious effort, and a strong desire to establish an environment of mutual trust.

An organizational assessment can be a two-edged sword. Without doing one, we are like a doctor prescribing medicine without examining the patient to determine what's really causing the symptoms. When an organization calls us and says, "We need training," our reaction is similar to that of a doctor whose patient calls and says, "I need antibiotics." If we do specifically what we are asked to, the likelihood is very high that the company will spend money and effort without getting the desired results.

On the other hand, when an assessment is done, people often have difficulty accepting the results. They can become defensive, deny the validity of the findings, or worse yet, shoot the messenger.

Objective evidence of return on investment

Assessments can do a number of things. They can pinpoint strengths and weaknesses, identify cultural and communication gaps, serve as a source of hard data to be used in the planning process, and provide a performance baseline against which future improvements can be measured. All too often we see performance-improvement efforts abandoned in a year or two because there is no objective evidence of a positive return on investment.

It's important to establish a baseline measurement of performance and to periodically measure progress against it. This will ensure continued support for the initiative and will provide a focus for improvement activities.

We suggest that an assessment be done at the onset of any major change effort, and that it be redone every 12-18 months thereafter. This is not to say that certain projects may not generate substantial improvement in a much shorter period of time, but it generally takes at least a year for a sustained series of ongoing improvements and real cultural change to begin to take place to any measurable degree.

This is a long time to wait for results, but by starting with an assessment, an organization knows it's taking the most direct route. The tendency is to jump in and form teams or to take other action before performing an assessment. Organizations that have taken this approach have found that performance improvements take far longer to achieve—if they are achieved at all.

A broad-based assessment provides measurements along the lines of what is sometimes referred to as a balanced scorecard. That is, it will help to guard against a change initiative that focuses so much attention on certain issues that things get out of balance, creating other problems.

An organization cannot realistically perform an assessment of itself. An objective viewpoint is needed, as well as the ability to quantify and evaluate the feedback.

Value of Baldridge criteria

For any company seeking a sound foundation and good overall direction for any substantial change effort, we wholeheartedly recommend the criteria for the Malcolm Baldridge National Quality Award (MBNQA). The Baldridge Award is one of the most prestigious and rigorous awards an American company can compete for. While the serious contenders are the most successful and experienced of companies, MBNQA has something important to offer every organization in search of high performance.

For one thing, the Baldridge criteria travel well. They are applicable to a variety of organizations and industries. Equally important, the criteria are the broadest and most comprehensive of all the standards we have encountered. They also enable us to *quantify* certain aspects of organizational performance that are otherwise very difficult to measure.

Leadership, for example, is absolutely critical to the success of any change effort. But what does appropriate leadership look like? How does that differ from the current leadership style? How large is the gap? How will the transition be made? And most important, how will progress be measured?

The Baldridge criteria can provide the answers to these kinds of questions. Furthermore, the MBNQA criteria are more comprehensive than other standards, including ISO and QS 9000.

The Baldridge criteria assessments have demonstrated to us time and time again that every organization is perfectly designed to achieve the results it gets. In other words, an organization cannot *accidentally* achieve consistently high levels of performance. An organization needs systems specifically designed to produce the desired results.

To achieve these kinds of results, an organization must focus on a defined set of core values that are part of a cohesive plan to achieve a measurable set of goals and objectives. Every company will need to clearly set forth its own specific set of values and goals, but the Baldridge criteria provide a good overall backdrop and an excellent benchmark against which to assess the current performance of the organization.

Baldridge core values and concepts

The Baldridge core values and concepts are straightforward and objective. They are as follows:

Customer-driven quality. Products and services demonstrably meet customers' needs rather than the organization's needs.

Leadership. Leaders clearly state their own vision and values, continuously reinforce these values, and model the behavior they expect of others.

Continuous improvement and learning. The organization focuses on constant innovation and adaptation rather than on following the rules and maintaining the status quo.

Employee participation and development. There is an understanding that performance depends on the skills and motivation of the workforce. An investment in workforce education is an investment in the future success of the organization.

Fast response. The organization recognizes that fast cycle times reduce cost and increase employee and customer satisfaction.

Design quality and prevention. The organization focuses on building quality into the product or service rather than getting good at detecting and correcting mistakes.

Long-range view. Leaders are willing to make long-term commitments to stakeholders.

Management by fact. Systems are created that make it easy for people at all levels in the organization to make decisions and to solve problems on the basis of objective data.

Partnership development. Internal and external alliances are built in order to achieve a competitive advantage.

Corporate responsibility and citizenship. The organization pays attention to the community as a stakeholder.

Results orientation. Everyone in the organization has access to full and current information about the organization's performance, presented as a balanced scorecard of performance indicators.

Through dedication to these core values, an organization will lay the foundation for integrating customer requirements and company performance. Most important, these core values help keep the focus on results.

The ideal high-performance organization

The core values above are embodied in all seven categories of the Baldridge criteria. The seven categories are given below, along with our vision of how each category would look in the ideal high-performance organization:

Leadership. Senior executives have a total commitment to performance excellence as demonstrated by a high level of personal involvement. They develop and maintain a strong management system. Customer focus and clear values and expectations are fully integrated into day-to-day operations. Leadership promotes performance excellence in all company activities. The values and expectations are also integrated into the company's management system that addresses both its public responsibilities and corporate citizenship.

Information and analysis. A well-managed and effective data base is used for planning, for day-to-day management, and for evaluation of continued improvement initiatives and success in the marketplace. Customer satisfaction, employee well-being, operational performance, and financial results are analyzed. This analysis is the basis of company-level review, corrective action, and improvement planning. Benchmarking of comparative data and information is used to support improvement of overall performance.

Strategic planning. A strategic planning process exists for overall performance and competitive leadership, and it addresses both the short and the long term. This plan leads to the development of key business drivers that serve as the basis for deploying the performance improvement plan throughout the organization. Major systems and improvement initiatives are aligned to support the achievement of the vision, goals, and objectives.

Human resource development and management. Plans and procedures for human resource development and management are in place and address all categories and types of employees. These practices maximize support for and contribute to the success of the company's performance improvement plans. Processes exist for recognition, reward, promotion, compensation, and feedback on performance; and they are consistent with the pursuit of customer satisfaction, employee well-being, and positive operational and financial results.

Process management. Processes are in place for the design and introduction of new or improved products and services. In addition, there are processes to assure that the organization meets key quality requirements and company performance goals. Production, delivery, support services, and general business processes are managed to ensure that current quality requirements are met and to create continuous improvement. Supplier quality is assured and is continuously improved through joint improvement initiatives. All business processes are continuously assessed.

Business results. Current product and service quality levels are equivalent to or better than those of the competition and are trending upward. Business processes, support services, and overall company operational performance exceed historical levels, those of the competition, and other appropriate benchmarks. Supplier quality levels exceed required minimums and are trending upward. Company operational and financial performance results are positive and are close to the performance improvement objectives.

Customer focus and satisfaction. The company is totally committed to customer satisfaction and continuous improvement. There are effectively managed relationships with customers, and the company uses objective data gained from customer feedback to determine customer satisfaction and to continuously improve quality and delivery performance. Customer satisfaction results exceed those of the competition and are trending upward. Future customer requirements and expectations are actively sought and translated into company strategic plans.

Cultural criteria

In addition to the Baldridge criteria, we have found five cultural criteria that need to be assessed to determine the kinds of cultural barriers that may need to be overcome in the implementation process. The following is our vision of how each of these criteria would look in the ideal high-performance organization.

Cooperation
- People understand and work together toward common goals which benefit everyone.

- Cooperation is evident between and among all groups—among managers, among people who work together, between managers and nonmanagement people, and between different departments or functions.
- When problems occur, people work together as a team to address and resolve them.

Empowerment
- Managers and supervisors routinely delegate responsibility and authority to the people who report to them.
- People have authority to take action on their own within clearly defined parameters without first consulting with a manager or supervisor.
- Many decisions are made by people below the manager level, and these people readily accept accountability for their decisions and actions.
- Employee teams make many decisions about how they will perform their work on a daily basis.

Communications
- Managers share as much information as they can with other employees about operational and other key issues.
- Managers and supervisors listen to the people who report to them and actively solicit their thoughts and ideas.
- Departments communicate effectively with each other.
- People are open and honest in communication with each other.
- There is effective two-way communication between people.

Trust
- People at all levels feel confident that others can and will carry out their duties in an effective manner.
- People believe that their managers are truthful and accurate in their communications, that there are no hidden agendas, and that managers can be depended on to carry out the commitments they make. Managers believe likewise about the people who report to them.
- A spirit of mutual respect exists between individuals and is exhibited in the way people interact in the course of daily business.

Innovation
- People are encouraged to try new or different approaches to solving problems and to improving operations.
- People are encouraged to be proactive when a situation arises which requires prompt action.
- People are encouraged to exercise initiative and to use new approaches.
- Failure is seen and used as an opportunity to learn rather than as a reason to punish.

As it creates a high-performance work system, an organization must address and improve along all of the above dimensions.

Common excuses and rationalizations

We have heard many excuses why companies don't want to base their improvement plans on objective assessment results: "We already know what our biggest problems are," or "It takes too much time," or "We don't want to raise expectations," or "It's too expensive," or "Our people don't understand what we face," or "It's too early," or "It's too late." The list goes on and on. Worse yet, some companies decide to do an assessment and then rationalize, deny, or just plain ignore the results.

No organization is perfect or ever will be. Striving continuously for perfection is the name of the game. In today's competitive world, if an organization is not continuously improving, it's falling behind the competition.

One of the first and most important steps to improving performance is to base improvements on an objective assessment of where the organization is now as compared to where it wants to be, and to use the results of the assessment to ensure that improvement efforts are designed to yield the desired performance results.

```
                              ↓
┌─────────────────────────────────────────────┐
│                                               │
│   **Leadership**                              │
│   1. Labor-Management Cooperation             │
│   2. Vision and Values                        │
│   3. Communication                            │
│   4. Compensation and Recognition             │
│   5. Change Management                        │
│   6. Role Model                               │
│                                               │
└─────────────────────────────────────────────┘
                              ↓
```

Any strategic initiative, particularly one that seeks to empower and involve the people of an organization in continuous performance improvement, must be led and supported from the top. It is vital that the leaders of the organization function well as a team, and that they be aware of their critical role in the implementation process. They should understand the need, the opportunity, the risk, the required resources, and the kind of personal change and commitment necessary to champion and to lead the process.

The concepts of continuous improvement, employee commitment, and the high-performance workplace cannot succeed without the support of people throughout the organization. Where there is a union, the union needs to be involved from the beginning and throughout the process. How can that happen, and how does it work in practice?

For generations, the relationship between labor and management in the U.S. could be described as adversarial at best. To talk about cooperation was considered foolish, even traitorous by some, and by others as just a waste of time.

Yet in the past several years, faced with global competition, leaders on both sides of the table have come to the realization that the old relationship does not serve either side well in today's economy.

Transition to a new way of doing things

Management and unions have begun to think about and to explore the possibility of working cooperatively to create performance improvement. WINOC has been involved with this subject since the early 1980s, when we began conducting workshops on the subject of labor-management cooperation for industrial audiences in various locations.

Some 2,000 people, a combination of managers and of employees represented by unions, have taken advantage of this opportunity to discuss the controversial topic of cooperation in a safe and neutral environment. These workshops have offered a critical view of the advantages and disadvantages, as well as the risks and benefits, of collaborative efforts to improve organizational performance. When people from several different companies come together to discuss these topics, we and they learn a great deal from each other.

Common goals

We have found that union and management have many goals in common. Both want a profitable company that will provide greater job security. Both want to satisfy customers. Both value pride in workmanship.

And, although in many cases both labor and management have been unable to figure out exactly how to achieve it, trust is also a common goal. There is a common desire for better communication upon which trust can be built. Managers and union members alike want to know where the company is headed, and both would rather work in an environment of cooperation than in one of constant adversarial behavior.

Getting ready for change

Common old scenarios must be rewritten if an organization is to break out of the old cycle of behavior. Scenarios such as the following are common: Management asks the union to be more flexible in regard to work rules and contract demands. The union suspects that this is part of a hidden agenda that will result in layoffs. Management asks employees to take on more responsibility for quality and for meeting customer expectations. Employees remember all the years when they offered ideas to management only to be ignored, and the union suspects that the acceptance of more responsibility will set people up for formal discipline.

The union says, "We will cooperate but we want a voice in developing a vision and in planning for the future. We know we can refine the work processes and contribute to the company's improvement efforts, but management needs to let us help implement the ideas."

Changing all this obviously cannot be accomplished in a short period of time. Later in this chapter we discuss in detail how to make change happen more smoothly.

Many union members and managers are still not ready for this move toward cooperation. The impetus for change needs to come from the top leaders on both sides. Just as a CEO cannot run an organization the same way in 1996 as in 1986 or 1976, neither can a union leader. Change is needed in order for any company to survive in today's competitive market.

Many companies and their unions have established joint cooperative efforts, several of which have been negotiated and spelled out in a special agreement known as a modern operating agreement. See, for example, the profiles in this book of L-S Electro-Galvanizing Company and of Ford Cleveland Engine Plant 2. Such agreements don't solve all the problems, but they do provide the groundwork for solid dialogue and change. See also the AFL-CIO publications in our Bibliography.

The Communication Workers of America and the International Brotherhood of Electrical Workers have also established some unique cooperative efforts within the communications industry. The International Association of Machinists and Aerospace Workers (IAM) has developed an approach called *Ten Steps to High Performance Work Organization Partnership*. The IAM offers joint union-management training sessions and encourages partnerships in which the union will have a real voice in operations.

Importance of training

As the workplace changes, a most important component is training and education for everyone, both labor and management. Until recently, very little training was available for those outside management aside from that aimed at teaching specific work skills.

A few years ago, the United Auto Workers and the big three U.S. auto-makers established a fund to support training at auto plants. A similar agreement has been made by the United Steel Workers of America and 13 major U.S. steel-producing companies.

When the top leaders of prominent corporations and the international unions work together, it sets the tone for cooperation in the companies represented by those unions. If proper training is provided, joint efforts at the local level provide local union presidents the education and training they need to properly support performance improvement initiatives. Similar training gives management staff the background they need to demonstrate appropriate support.

For union and management leaders, it's a matter of jointly walking the talk, of setting an example by how they conduct themselves in the course of their day-to-day business.

First steps on a long journey

Experience shows us that it's a long journey from the way things are to the way things need to be. At first, the exploration of these new cooperative work systems may entail as many steps backward as forward. The foundation of trust, which we discussed in the first chapter, may be new and very fragile. Labor-management cooperation may seem to be an unrealistic expectation, but we have seen over and over again that it is an essential prerequisite to high performance.

Cooperation is a byproduct of trust, and trust is built on effective communications. Communications are enhanced as labor and management leaders, following our change model, identify common interests, needs, and values. As leaders incorporate these into a shared vision of the future, several things happen. The common ground between labor and management begins to increase. This results in a greater level of trust, which fosters further cooperation. As the leaders jointly communicate the vision and solicit the support and commitment of others, their cooperation serves as a role model for the rest of the organization.

What will inspire and motivate people to accept more responsibility, to identify opportunities, and to take on new challenges? A powerful vision will. It provides guidance for decisions, meaning for work, focus for improvements, and the basis for setting priorities.

Creating a vision is a required step in developing a Long-Range Performance Improvement Plan. But part of the problem for many organizations is that they develop a vision only because they think they are supposed to. The result is a soulless and meaningless statement that could be transported to any other organization.

Here's a typical example: "The ABC Company strives to be a world-class organization. Our employees are committed to excellence as we meet or exceed our customers' expectations." By simply changing the name, one could transport this statement to any organization—not that it would serve any useful purpose.

This kind of vision statement fails to relay what management really wants to achieve. It is just an awkward, wordy statement that tries to capture the universe but ends up mouthing generalizations and gathering dust on the wall in the lobby.

Signs of fuzzy vision

A fuzzy, nonproductive vision is manifested in many ways in the daily life of an organization. Here are some signs of a poor vision:
- A rumor mill is active.
- There is frequent disagreement about priorities.
- People are pessimistic about the future or cynical about the present.
- People are reluctant to accept responsibility or new tasks.
- Some people seem to be working only for a paycheck.
- It's necessary to closely supervise how work is done.
- Management has difficulty describing the benefits of the organization's continuous-improvement activities.

The more "yes" answers, the more an organization's vision needs correction.

A call for action

A quality vision statement serves a useful purpose. It describes the future. It provides direction. It creates a vivid picture of what the organization wants to be in the future. It gets people's hearts beating a little faster. It serves as a call to action.

One of the best vision statements was reputed to be that of Komatsu, a Japanese manufacturer of construction machines, whose vision statement was said to be, "Kill Caterpillar!"

Perhaps this story is more legend than fact. Some may disagree with the sentiment. And if the story is true, Komatsu probably had a different, more diplomatic vision statement on display in its lobby. But that statement has laserlike focus. Everyone in the organization can understand it and work toward it. And it certainly boosts the adrenaline.

A vision statement can be less bloodthirsty yet still as effective. For example, a group of managers for a defense contractor was struggling to develop a vision statement. When the group was challenged to come up with something vivid and unique, one manager said, "The central issue is that none of our talk about excellence and commitment matters one bit if Congress doesn't buy our new system." Then he said: "We have to be quick enough, flexible enough, cost-effective enough, and produce such high quality that Congress is left with no choice but to vote for this system." Now *that* is a vision statement!

Criteria for a vision statement

Here are key attributes of an effective vision statement. Test your organization's vision against these criteria:

- It drives new modes of action and forces choices. It is dissonant with what the organization has done in the past. It very obviously is very different from business as usual.
- It provokes response and interest. People ask questions like: How on earth can we do that? Why are we going in that direction? What's my part in all that?
- It is clear and concise. This is not to say that it's totally self-explanatory. It should get people talking, and it should especially get leaders talking to everyone else in the organization.

A strong vision is the foundation of empowerment, which is the key to continuous improvement.

A vision statement is not a tool for public relations or marketing. It is a tool for internal use. By contrast, a mission statement describes the organization's purpose and is designed for external use.

Vision at work

An organization that focuses clearly on its vision is using a powerful tool that will drive a successful strategy of performance improvement. Shaping an effective vision requires time and effort, but it is absolutely essential. We call attention to the following:

Consensus among leaders. Leadership must reach consensus on core values: the ideals, customs, and beliefs that deal with the way the business is run. A facilitator begins this process by listing some things that all managers must pay attention to, such as planning (goal-setting), problem-solving and decision-making, communications, collaboration, managing agreement and conflict, developing human resources, motivation, and innovation. The leaders identify their beliefs in relation to these issues and to their personal values. For example, one goal may be increased profit; its corresponding value describes how that goal will be pursued, such as through highly participative management.

Values will determine how everything is done. They can vary widely from one organization to another. For example, in an inherently dangerous environment, safety must be a primary value. Values serve to measure the rightness of the vision. People have an emotional attachment to their values, and personal values may not mesh with the organization's values. It's important, therefore, to reach consensus on these issues, a process that often takes a considerable length of time. We discuss consensus in the chapters on conflict resolution and creative problem-solving.

Involvement of everyone. The major stakeholders must be brought into the visioning process: employees, unions, owners, stockholders. A vision established in a collaborative way will become a much greater source of energy and effectiveness. Sometimes a very strong leader will have a well-defined vision and will articulate it with great conviction. But such a vision belongs exclusively to the leader. For a vision to be effective, everyone has to feel ownership.

If employees are represented by a union, its leaders should be involved as soon as possible in the development of the vision. The visioning process cannot succeed without their active support and participation both in planning and in implementation.

Alignment with the environment. At this point the vision is expanded by using information about the realities surrounding the business—an assessment of strengths, weaknesses, opportunities, and threats.

Awareness of paradigms. It's important to make certain that the vision is not limited by paradigms, those self-imposed constraints that exist in the mind but not in reality. The ideal is an open mind!

Maintaining perspective. A successful organization doesn't throw out the baby with the bathwater. Leaders appreciate what has been achieved in the past and retain what was positive and effective. At the same time they take full advantage of the opportunities the future represents.

Fulfillment of needs

The work of an organization and of its people can fulfill many needs; two of the most significant are job security and meaningful work. A clear vision of the future and a commitment to that vision are the basis for fulfilling these needs.

In the implementation of high-performance work systems, too little attention tends to be paid to ongoing communication of progress toward the vision and values. It's hard work, and time-consuming. But just as the saying goes, "If you don't measure it, you can't improve it," an important corollary is also true, namely, "If you don't communicate it, it won't happen."

Because performance improvement involves significant changes, the vision and values need to be communicated to everyone in the organization.

Challenges for communication

Creating a high-performance work system will require communication that successfully meets these four challenges:
1. to create an atmosphere of trust in an era of widespread corporate downsizing,
2. to provide a sense of direction in a time of great uncertainty,
3. to create a long-term strategy instead of a short-term program, and
4. to recognize people fairly and to avoid alienating groups or individuals.

Create an atmosphere of trust

Trust was discussed earlier in the context of corporate culture. Suffice it to say here that consistency is the key. It's absolutely essential to follow through on commitments and to make certain that words and deeds are always mutually supportive. If any given situation requires actions that may be perceived as inconsistent, these actions should be explained fully to those people who are affected. It should not be assumed that people will understand, particularly if all the relevant information has not been shared with them.

Provide a sense of direction

The announcement of any change initiative needs to be supported by specific information about why change is needed, what those changes will be, and where the organization is headed. These specifics are necessary in order to obtain employee commitment to the change process. Lacking such specifics, a general announcement typically results in more uncertainty and skepticism.

Timing of the communication is important. In an effort to communicate, some companies make a general announcement prematurely, before a vision has been formulated, and say only, "We need to change and improve, so we want everyone to get involved in improving performance."

The result is a mixed message. Lacking specifics, it creates confusion because nobody knows how or what to change, and it creates doubt about management's intentions. A further likelihood is that people will go off in all sorts of directions exerting a lot of effort. But without focus or direction, these efforts may cancel each other out and fail to result in any real improvement.

Create a long-term strategy

We all have a tendency to attach labels to new concepts. The problem with this tendency is that all too often concepts are named and announced, and then left unsupported by action. People are quick to recognize such concepts as the program-of-the-month. Concepts, slogans, and labels all tend to be perceived as just more short-lived hype.

Although most people seem to resist labels, they do support concepts. They do want to get involved in improving work processes and increasing customer satisfaction.

A word about programs: a program, even if it is a bona fide one, is by nature short-term. It has a beginning and an end. A high-performance strategy is very different. It is a permanent commitment to a change, a change in the way business is done. A common thread running through our *Profiles* is the awareness of this difference and the communication to people in the organization that high performance is a long-term strategy.

Recognize people fairly

Recognition is part of the essential step of communicating the organization's progress. It's not enough for management to encourage employee involvement and to take action on recommendations for improvement. It's also important to communicate when the suggestions have helped to achieve the goals and, at that point, to recognize teams and individuals for their contributions.

What incentives do all employees have for developing commitment to the change strategy and for working together to improve performance? It's essential to link the reward system to the vision, values, and goals.

When it comes to compensation, people are understandably very protective. They know how much is supposed to be in their paycheck, and they tend to be very suspicious of any efforts to modify the compensation system in any way.

Most companies have a rigid pay structure, with job classifications, pay grades and ranges, and lots of rules. The organizational structure is equally rigid, with job descriptions, work procedures, and policies which tend to focus people's attention on the performance of their individual job responsibilities. This kind of structure builds in very few incentives to work together to improve quality and productivity or to support a long-range change strategy.

One strategy and approach

When AT&T decided to go into the credit-card business in 1990, it faced a formidable challenge. Because consumers were already inundated with credit-card choices, AT&T knew its Universal Card could be successful only if it provided extraordinary customer service. AT&T realized that its people needed motivation to stay focused on the goal of extraordinary service. AT&T began the development of its reward system by asking two basic questions:
1. What specifically do we want to achieve?
2. What reward strategy will work best to help us do that?

After the goals and the approach were clarified, company leaders developed a compensation system designed to reward employees for the achievement of specific objectives.

To keep people focused on the goals, leaders spelled out several quality indicators and specific objectives for each indicator. Part of every person's compensation is tied to the achievement of these quality objectives. Bonuses are paid quarterly and are as much as 20% of base pay.

The new system is working. Everyone understands the mission and knows what he or she must do to support it.

Types of systems in use

American companies have been experimenting with a variety of innovative compensation systems designed to complement base compensation with rewards and recognition for outstanding performance. Most of these systems offer employees a stable package of base pay and benefits and then add a variable component. This variable component can range all the way from nonfinancial recognition to sophisticated financial incentives. The list includes such things as:

Suggestion plans. Individuals or groups are paid a percentage of the savings generated from improvement ideas.

Recognition programs. Certificates, tokens of appreciation, newsletter stories, honorary awards, or even preferred parking spots are given for individual or group performance.

Small-group incentives. Financial bonuses are given uniformly to all members of a group for achieving a predetermined objective.

Pay for performance. Pay is based on individual performance.

Pay for knowledge. Pay increases are based on the number of skills or jobs mastered.

Profit sharing. A predetermined percentage of pre-tax profit is paid to all participating employees.

Gain sharing. A percentage of gains, or improvements, over a predetermined baseline is shared with all participating employees.

How to get started

It's essential to form a broadly representative leadership group to develop and oversee the new approach to reward and recognition. This group should:
1. Study the alternatives that have been used in other companies.
2. Make a thorough assessment of the current system of reward and recognition.
3. Make an appraisal of the key business objectives and the company's ability to measure them.

Gain sharing

This is an excellent vehicle for aligning performance with rewards and for reinforcing employee involvement and continuous improvement. Gain sharing is a financial reward system that pays bonuses for progress toward goals as measured against baseline performance. Gains are measured by a predetermined formula, which is usually developed by an employee committee with the help of a gain sharing expert.

Gain sharing complements teamwork but, more than that, the success of gain sharing depends on the organization having a system that enables employees to create gains, or improvements. Gain sharing is ineffective in a traditional management structure because it lacks such a system.

Because a gain sharing system often includes measurement of nonfinancial indicators, there is the possibility that bonuses could be paid even when there are no profits. Accordingly, in designing a company's gain sharing system, it's important to select appropriate measurements of performance that tie into the strategic goals and that will ultimately have an impact on financial performance.

Gain sharing has certain advantages over profit sharing. Profit sharing is tied to a line of net profit on the profit-and-loss statement, which is influenced by many factors beyond the control of most employees. By contrast, gain sharing is generally tied to performance that is within the control of most employees.

Also, profit sharing is paid infrequently, usually annually or semiannually, and payment can be in noncash form, such as a contribution to a retirement fund. By contrast, gain sharing is almost always paid in cash on a monthly or quarterly basis so that people get timely feedback on the effectiveness of what they are doing.

It's true that the design of a gain sharing system can be fairly complex and needs to be customized to the organization. And it's important to educate all employees about the system, what it will reward, and how it relates to their work.

Rewards for the organization

Linking the reward and recognition system to long-term company goals is a key step in aligning the interests of its people. If the system is tied to appropriate measurements, and if people have the ability to make improvements in those factors measured by the plan, then gain sharing can provide the missing link between the performance of the organization and the efforts of its people.

In addition to the changes needed to incorporate high-performance work systems, organizations also face the realization that change will continue to accelerate in other areas. There are ways to manage this change with a minimum amount of pain.

It's human nature to resist change. Change is often difficult to cope with, and it's difficult to direct. But to survive and thrive as a business, it is inescapable.

Common responses to change

Initial attempts to involve employees in performance improvement may be fraught with various kinds of subtle resistance. Perhaps the following attitudes may sound familiar:

"It's their fault, not mine." Managers or supervisors may blame their subordinates for failure to make progress toward the achievement of goals. In reality, the managers or supervisors may have little ownership in the concept and may be reluctant to make the necessary changes in their own behavior.

"What's good for the company is good for me." Some managers or supervisors have ceased to think or act individually. Instead, they act entirely from an organizational perspective, going along with whatever view the company presents. As a result they screen the information they give to top management and project a less-than-accurate picture of the work situation to match their perception of top management's expectations. While acting as if they support the concepts, they may be merely talking the talk in order to meet their boss' expectations. Such superficial acceptance is actually a hindrance. It can stifle creativity, innovation, and spontaneity in the workforce. If not dealt with, it can sabotage successful performance improvement.

"I'll wait it out. This too shall pass." People at any level may be unwilling to perform new tasks, assume new roles, or change their behavior. Only when top management constantly and consistently backs up its words with actions, do people realize that change has indeed arrived.

"I'll pretend to go along with it." People who seem to be in agreement may be suppressing their actual feelings. Sometimes people will be reluctant to express disagreement openly. But it's important to encourage individuals to express their concerns. Only after people have articulated and worked through their concerns will they be ready and able to move on to the new ideas and behaviors.

Ways to better manage change

Here are three strategies to minimize the natural resistance to change:

Communicate in advance. Nobody likes surprises. People need to know about the change in advance. They need to know why a change is being made and how it will affect them. Advance communication reduces uncertainty and the resistance that almost always accompanies it.

Many companies withhold information about upcoming change for fear of upsetting employees. The opposite usually happens: people feel angry or suspicious. Anger fuels resistance and makes the change more difficult to implement. Also, imaginations work overtime and the rumor mills become active; if people aren't told the reasons for change, they will invent their own.

Counteract such problems by giving factual information as early as possible. Doing so acknowledges that employees have a stake in the change. People treated as adults will respond as adults.

Involve people. When people at any level of an organization are isolated from the planning and implementation of change, they perceive the change as belonging to someone else. When people can participate in change instead of having it imposed upon them, they will have a sense of ownership.

Because people are almost always affected by change, they should be involved as much as possible by means of planning committees, task forces, and change implementation teams. They can be asked for input individually as well as in groups. It's hard for any of us to resist our own ideas.

Implement change in small increments. When people are learning something new, they can acquire only a limited amount of information at one time. And they do it in steps. We learn how to add and subtract before tackling advanced mathematics.

Successful change involves learning. Change is best carried out amidst a great deal of communication, interaction, participation, involvement, and sharing of ideas and information.

When large changes are introduced in rapid-fire manner, unaccompanied by information, people get overloaded and resist.

By introducing change with sufficient information, an organization is using a powerful method of generating acceptance and understanding. This may slow things down somewhat, but deliberate planning and early communication will pay dividends in results later on.

With all the changes that organizations must make to stay competitive, the ability to manage change effectively becomes increasingly important. Whether the change is a technological change or a process change, these few simple principles will enable the change efforts to bear fruit more quickly and with far less pain.

A new kind of leadership is needed to convey and nurture the vision of excellence, to unleash the powerful people-potential within a company, and to serve as a change agent in complex systems designed to support the status quo.

In its simplest form, leadership is the process of influencing people in a positive direction. When an organization decides to pursue a strategy of performance improvement, a major shift is required in the organization's culture and work style—and in the pattern of that organization's leadership in support of this change. It is the leader's responsibility to model this behavior.

Lead, follow, *and* get out of the way

High-performance leadership is not for the timid, the lukewarm, or the half-hearted. It's a parachute jump. It requires a level of commitment, enthusiasm, and faith that one too rarely finds in senior executives-which is why so many leaders view it more as a jump from the top of a skyscraper.

"Lead, follow, or get out of the way," is a popular quotation ascribed to General Patton and to contemporary leaders such as Lee Iacocca and others who undoubtedly expressed it more colorfully and forcefully. Make one small but all-important change in that quotation, and it is transformed into a succinct summary of a successful high-performance leadership style: "Lead, follow, *and* get out of the way."

Lead

Leaders must be strong. They must set high standards and must not compromise them. Strong leadership is essential for high performance because the required changes must be implemented in a highly focused way throughout the organization. The alternative— people working in isolated pockets within their own work areas—can result in little or no impact on the organization as a whole or, worse yet, its impact can even be detrimental.

If the leader sets the pace and walks the talk, people will begin to believe the leader really means business. For example, one of the most autocratic of managers in one of the toughest of environments became convinced that he needed to change his style. He told his people, "I anticipate that there will be three types of reaction to this change. Some of you will love the new way, and that's great. A lot of you will sit back and watch and not interfere, and that's okay. And others of you may decide that you no longer want to work here."

In *Flight of the Buffalo*, James Belasco describes why the leader must change first. The leader lays down behavioral tracks, showing people where to go and what to do. Each leader on down the chain repeats that pattern. The signals have been sent telling what good behavior looks like.

Follow

Leaders need to demonstrate openness to input and feedback—even negative—from their subordinates. What is openness? It's a willingness on the part of leaders to listen to the perceptions and ideas of others, even when these ideas and perceptions don't match their own. Openness is the ability to be flexible and to try someone else's ideas. Openness is essential in the shaping of the vision, in the creation of strategies to solve problems, and in the implementation of suggestions for improvement. Leaders need to ask questions of their people, to listen to the answers, and to respond in a way that says, "I hear you, and your thought is valid."

What happens when a leader asks employees, "What about my leadership style bothers you most?" Bob Galvin of Motorola asked his people that question. The most frequent response was that he was inaccessible. His secretary screened his calls so thoroughly that if an employee managed to get through, it was often too late. In response, Bob Galvin committed to do these things:
1. to answer his own phone,
2. to answer by the third ring, and
3. to chart and to post his performance.

Then he went back to the employees and asked, "How am I doing?" He accomplished three important things in the process:
1. he took action on what his people told him,
2. he made a visible change that made a difference, and
3. he paved the way for future openness between him and his people.

It's important to walk the talk. Consider what a leader actually tells people when he or she says, "I support your decision to pursue this strategy, but I retain the right to veto it." People perceive everything said before the "but" as being untrue. That leader is really saying, "You people change first, and then I'll decide if I'm going to change." That doesn't work.

Leadership for high performance is all about delegation of authority and responsibility, but the one thing that cannot be delegated is leadership itself. A leader must personally be involved in the process. Leaders must support decisions made at the lowest possible levels of the organization and, whenever possible, decisions should be made by consensus.

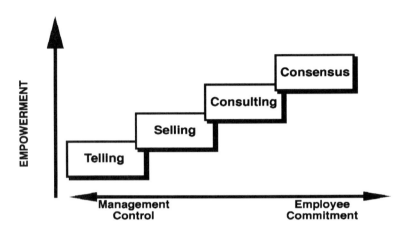

Skip Lefauve, the President of Saturn Corporation, summarizes the four types of decision-making.
1. Telling: "This is what you'll do."
2. Selling: "Here's why we want to do this."
3. Consulting: "What do you think?"
4. Consensus: "What can we all live with and support?"

Consensus almost always takes longer, but it results in a better decision and one that's easier and faster to implement because people have a sense of ownership in it. Some decisions have to be made in one of the other modes, but good leaders make sure that the important decisions are made through consensus. We say more about consensus in the chapters on conflict resolution and creative problem-solving.

Get out of the way!

To really empower their subordinates, leaders have to bite their tongues. They have to allow people the freedom to make mistakes and to learn from them. Leaders have to give people the tremendous pleasure of really running with the ball under their own power.

That's easier said than done! It requires not only the delegation of decision-making authority but also a lot of planning and training for employees. To a great extent, American corporations have done a lot of talking about this style of leadership but have not frequently succeeded in implementing it.

There are many things leaders can do to get out of the way and encourage people in the organization to take a more active role. Here are some helpful ways to begin doing this:

1. Do more listening and less talking in meetings.
2. Next, stay out of the meetings completely.
3. Start pushing problems back to people when they present them rather than solving the problems for them.
4. Help others do rather than doing for them.
5. Keep in mind that there's too much to know and to do, and too much competition, for any one person to know all the answers.

Belasco says that one of the most difficult things for a leader to do is to change his behavior to allow people to take ownership. He also says that learning how to let others lead is vital for success.

When the leader gets out of the way, people can take ownership. Equally important, the leader's new behavior serves as a role model for others throughout the organization. When the boss' behavior changes, nobody's behavior or job stays the same.

```
            ↓
┌─────────────────────────────────────┐
│                                      │
│   **Performance Improvement Plan**   │
│   1. Key Result Areas                │
│   2. Goals                           │
│   3. Stretch Goals                   │
│   4. Measurement                     │
│   5. Plan Development                │
│   6. Implementation                  │
│                                      │
└─────────────────────────────────────┘
            │
```

A performance improvement plan begins with a vision of the future which incorporates the values of the leadership group. Based on an assessment of the gap between the vision of the future and the realities of the present, specific goals and measurable objectives are developed to bridge the gap. An action plan is then incorporated to communicate the vision, goals, and objectives, and to solicit ideas, or tactics, from the entire workforce on how to achieve the vision. The vision, goals, objectives, tactics, and associated measurements are what we refer to as the performance improvement plan.

Key Result Areas

We have found that three key result areas can serve very effectively as the framework for the performance improvement plan of almost any organization. These areas probably will sound familiar. They're mentioned in most books and articles on the subject, so at first glance these areas may seem too broad or too vague, but they can work wonders as the foundation of any plan. These key result areas are:

- customer satisfaction,
- employee satisfaction and well-being, and
- positive financial and operational performance.

Within each area, the organization should identify key performance indicators, or measurements, and specific measurable goals. Goals are then broken down into objectives, which are more specific, and finally into even more specific tactics, or ideas for improvement. These key result areas have four strong advantages:

They are basic. Just about everything an organization seeks to accomplish can be categorized into one of these three areas. They cover nearly all interests of an organization, including the financial ones.

They travel well. These goals apply to all organizations, including those in hospitality, manufacturing, health care, and the public sector. And within a given organization, they apply to all functions and to all departments.

They are measurable. Most organizations are already tracking some key indicators in each of these key result areas. Existing reports may not be totally adequate, so new ones may need to be developed, but it's generally not difficult to do. Finally, these areas provide the foundation for the development of a pyramid of measurements—in other words, micro-indicators that can be traced to macro-measures. Accounting measures are a good example of indicators that pyramid— a common thread can connect the amount of money spent on paper for copying machines to the yearly profit realized by the organization.

They are strategic. We have found that organizations that achieve superior results in these three areas also do well in the marketplace.

Customer satisfaction

When deciding where to dedicate resources for improvement, leadership should prioritize areas important to the customer. Much of what we see organizations measure is unimportant to the customer. Total production volume is an example of a performance measurement that has traditionally received more attention than it deserves. Two other examples are labor and equipment utilization rates. These are measurements that have traditionally been used as barometers of manufacturing efficiency.

But if labor is busy performing non-value-adding work such as stocking and moving material, inspecting, or reworking, then the only thing being added is cost. Similarly, if machines are busy producing poor-quality products or parts that will go into stock, machine utilization is not a good indicator of efficiency.

Some indicators may seem to be customer-oriented but really aren't. Consider for example Smith Widgets, which has several sites from which it ships widgets to customers. Smith decided that a good measure of customer satisfaction was on-time delivery performance, defined as the percentage of an order that Smith ships on or before the promised delivery date.

Smith was proud of its on-time delivery performance, which was 95% or better at most of its sites. But when Smith began communicating more closely with its customers, it found that many customers were actually frustrated by Smith's delivery system.

When Smith received an order, it was often split among warehouses in different divisions. Each division may have shipped 100% of its order on time. But the customer could receive part of the order on Monday from the eastern division, another part on Wednesday from the western division, and the final part on Friday from the southern division—and separate invoices from each division.

Another example: Jones Company set a goal of getting its bids out within 10 days. It measured that goal and was proud of meeting it 99% of the time. But the company later discovered that customers considered 10 days too long.

Employee satisfaction and well-being

Each of the three key result areas is interrelated and has a direct impact on the others. The prevailing wisdom is that improvement activities all need to start with and be focused on customers. The corollary is that employees will derive satisfaction from their ability to contribute and will derive security from the company's enhanced viability.

In general we find this to be true. However, as discussed earlier in issues of corporate culture, if there is deep-seated mistrust or a great deal of dissatisfaction at the start, these issues need to be addressed directly, before proceeding with anything else, or they will continue to interfere with the improvement activities.

We have also found some leaders who feel very strongly that employee satisfaction must be the first priority, on the premise that if an organization first devotes its attention to employee satisfaction, the employees in turn will do whatever is necessary to ensure customer satisfaction. Suffice it to say that strong relationships exist among all three areas, and the absolute first priority is to at least neutralize employee dissatisfaction.

Positive financial and operational performance

American managers are notoriously impatient, and our traditional management style is geared to short-term results. It's hard to convince American managers that there is value in strategies like the pursuit of high performance because such strategies are rooted in long-range plans for incremental improvement.

So we find that change initiatives are often implemented by jumping right into teams, random problem-solving, or the improvement of small work processes. This usually results in one of two outcomes, neither of which is good. If the first attempt at improvement fails, then the entire strategy often takes the blame and is abandoned.

If the first attempt succeeds—which it easily can, particularly if it's the only improvement activity and gets a lot of initial attention—then there is the tendency to start more and more projects. Ultimately this too will fail due to the lack of an overall sense of direction, too few resources, resistance to change, misalignment of major systems, too little training, low employee morale, or any of a number of other factors that need to be anticipated and dealt with up front.

An initial demonstration project

Starting with one planned demonstration project is a compromise approach that we have found can succeed under the right circumstances. If the right project is selected, the savings can begin to fund the training and other expenses of implementation.

The project that seems best suited for this purpose is the reduction of setup times. There is a definite procedure to be followed, employee involvement is essential, and dramatic tangible results normally can be achieved in a relatively short period of time, usually in two to three months at about one hour per week. The purpose of such a project is to allow a group of people to experience first-hand how improvements can be made and to demonstrate to the rest of the organization what can be accomplished.

The trappings of high performance are often confused with its essentials, and what needs to be done is more easily understood than how it should be done or in what sequence. Teams, work redesign, and employee recognition are all important, but goal-setting must be done first. The nature of the goals will determine the nature of the activity. Goals should be clear, specific, measurable, and challenging. In order to ensure this, the following steps should be taken.

Identify the destination

High-performance organizations employ a number of techniques, including—but not limited to—the establishment and training of employee teams, the development of ways to gather and act on employee ideas, and the creation of systems to recognize employee efforts.

While all these methods are valid, they are the tools of the strategy, not its ends. Before leaping onto the horse and galloping off, it's important to decide on the destination: the company's vision and goals.

Properly used, performance improvement tools will produce results, but many of the false starts and failed efforts are the result of plunging ahead with the use of these tools before setting clear goals. Measurable goals will provide a company with a competitive advantage over those organizations that don't employ them and over those organizations that plunge into improvement activities without a clear sense of direction.

Separate the means from the ends

All too often, we find teams whose mission is "to improve communications." Certainly, nobody objects to such activity, and that's one of the problems with it: it's viewed as harmless, and all will agree to it as proof that they support the improvement process. But it's a waste of time and energy to establish a team with such a broad objective. There should be evidence of a specific problem and an objective way to measure the effectiveness of the team's work.

Similarly, we have seen too many plans that specify how many teams will be established but that fail to state what the teams should be chartered to do. Moreover, these plans often call for the infliction of hours of training on skeptical employees without first identifying what the training is intended to accomplish and how its effectiveness will be evaluated.

Measure results, not activity

Many organizations find themselves engaged in great amounts of activity aimed at creating high performance, but in reality that activity has virtually no impact at all on the factors critical to the success of the organization. In such situations, there is a telling absence of any basic measures of overall performance improvement.

High activity does *not* equal high performance.

The more focused the activity is on the organization's key goals, the more impact it will have. While the pursuit of high performance can be a lot of work, focused improvement activities can produce results fully commensurate with the effort expended.

Set goals with sharp focus

If high performance is to be achieved, leadership must have a clear vision of what needs to be improved. No organization needs improvement activity per se, but all organizations have a need to improve, even companies that have already achieved very high levels of performance. Successful organizations continuously analyze internal and external customer needs and then carefully define those things that need to be improved.

Goals must be translated into areas of precise focus. When initiatives are kicked off with a general directive to "go forth and continuously improve," the tendency is for everyone to go back to the workplace and do what they have always been doing. After all, nobody wants to think they don't always try to do their best. This may actually be preferable to the alternative reaction, which is to make random changes, suboptimizing individual functions.

Set stretch goals

It's also important to set stretch goals: performance targets that are *way* out there. As Jack Welch, CEO of General Electric, says, "If you set a performance goal and you can figure out how you are going to get there, it's not much of a goal." It's easy to identify a stretch goal: employee reactions will be, "That's impossible!" or "You must be joking!"

Provide for measurement

After answering, "What exactly do we want to see improved?" the next question to ask is, "How will we know if it's improving?" Good measurement indicators can sharpen focus on fuzzy goals.

For example, "to improve communication" is a fuzzy goal. But if an employee survey is developed and used on a regular basis, it can more clearly define and measure what is meant by the word communication. If the survey shows that only 40% of all employees say they get adequate feedback on job performance from their supervisors, then the company can give supervisors training in effective feedback skills. If 70% of all employees later report adequate feedback on job performance, the company can confidently state that the training achieved its intended result.

Signals that efforts are out of sync

All too often we hear questions which tell us that an organization's performance improvement efforts are ineffective. When these questions are voiced, it's time to stop for a moment, evaluate what's really happening, and develop a corrective plan.

"How can we get buy-in?" This question indicates that implementation got underway before the leadership developed the necessary ownership in the plans for improvement. Leadership should back up, open up to possible alternatives, and involve those people whose support and participation are critical to the success of the plans.

"How can we measure the impact?" This question indicates that activities were begun without regard to how they might impact a specific goal or measurable objective—or even before specific goals were set. When this question is asked, chances are that little, if any, impact will be found. Leadership should back up, establish measurable goals and objectives, and then charter activities designed to achieve those goals.

"What kind of training do teams need and how much?" If this question is asked early on, it usually indicates that teams have been equated with high performance, or that there is the belief that high activity will produce high performance. Leadership should back up, ensure that teams are designed to help achieve specific goals, and then train teams in the tools and techniques needed to produce the specific results they have been chartered to achieve.

"How can we implement this process and run the business at the same time?" This question indicates two problems. The improvement process is not focused on critical issues, and traditional business systems haven't changed enough to facilitate the implementation. Leadership should back up and re-evaluate the goals as well as the implementation plan. High performance represents change in the way the business is run. There will always be resistance to change, but if the need to change is critical and if people have ownership in the means to achieve the change, then people will find the time.

The first obstacle encountered when setting stretch goals—those goals that go beyond the organization's perception of its capability—is getting leaders to set goals that they don't already think they know how to achieve. Successful pursuit of stretch goals requires faith in people, and a culture that supports experimentation and innovation rather than one that breeds conservatism and fear of failure.

The hammer-and-anvil syndrome

Stretch goals are tough to support, tough to pursue, and tough to get people to commit to. One reason is what we call the hammer-and-anvil syndrome.

In traditional cultures, performance targets serve as the anvil, and measurements serve as the hammer used to obtain performance improvement. If the goals fail to be achieved, bewildered managers are told, "If you can't do it, we'll find someone who can." If they exceed the goals, they are asked, "Why haven't you been performing at this level all along?" This is obviously a no-win situation. So it's not surprising that people often view performance targets, especially stretch targets, with a lot of skepticism.

If dramatic performance improvement is to become a way of doing business, a different environment must be created.

In the hammer-and-anvil environment, performance is either good or bad, depending on where it stands relative to the target. If the indicator shows that performance is under the goal, a search for suspects is conducted and the guilty parties are admonished. If the indicator shows that performance has exceeded the goal, a variety of actions may occur, often with less-than-optimum results.

Setting stretch goals

The setting of stretch goals begins in this way:

Identify a few broad business processes. Some examples are order entry to product delivery; getting a patient from the emergency room to a hospital bed; or new product design to production.

Measure current performance. How long does it take? How many errors occur? What is the cost?

Set ambitious performance targets. These targets should actually seem unreasonable in terms of current performance. They therefore necessitate work redesign rather than incremental improvement.
Identify and provide the necessary resources. This doesn't necessarily mean allocating a lot of money or hiring more staff. To pursue stretch goals, people need information, training, authority, trust, time, and receptivity to ideas.

Required: a new leadership style

With traditional leadership, management's interaction with employees tends to vary greatly according to whether performance is above or below the goal. This practice is nonproductive, particularly with stretch goals. Behavior should be similar regardless of the level of performance.

For example, let's visit Smith Widgets again. Its stated goal is to improve customer satisfaction, with one indicator being the on-time delivery performance. The specific objective was to improve the performance from its existing average of 72% to a stretch goal of 95%. The eastern division had a mediocre performance of 75%; the western division actually beat the target, improving its performance to 96%.

Joe Jones, the senior vice president of operations, reviewed these figures at the end of the quarter and, true to his traditional leadership style, rounded up all the guilty parties, namely the managers in the eastern division, and read them the riot act for not making more improvement. He also invited all the heroes in the western division to a celebration dinner and congratulated them on reaching the goal.

Shortly afterward, Jones was replaced by Diane Davis, who also decided to address delivery performance with all the division managers. Her conversations, however, were very similar with both groups. First, she referred to the specific goal and displayed the charts of delivery performance for the quarter.

In her meeting with the eastern division managers, she said, "As you are aware, the delivery performance for this division is currently at 75%, which represents only a 4% increase over the past few months. First, let's list all potential causes of poor delivery performance, and then we'll prioritize those causes. Finally, let's all agree that no potential change is off limits, and I'll commit to try whatever ideas you come up with. Let's get started. I'm confident that we can reach our stated goal."

When she met with the eastern division managers, she said, "As you can see, the delivery performance for this division is currently at 96%, after a very good 33% improvement over the past few months. That's a fine job. We've achieved the goal, and I'm sure we can do even better. First, we'll list all the things that are still barriers to performance, and then we'll prioritize the stubborn ones. Finally, let's all agree that nothing is off limits, and I'll commit to at least try any new ideas. I'm confident that we can improve these results even further!"

Joe's leadership style is not only a barrier to improvement, but it also makes it very unlikely that managers will ever support or commit to stretch goals again. On the other hand, Diane's style creates a culture of dramatic improvement through innovation. She recognizes that admonishing people for failure to achieve stretch goals and over-rewarding good performance will only serve to limit performance improvement over the long run. Further, she recognizes that performance generally has more to do with systems than it does with human performance within those systems.

She knows that hammering managers will not result in the achievement of stretch goals. She has found that significant performance improvement is brought about by engaging people in identifying systems problems and by giving them the authority to completely rethink those systems, without regard to any sacred cows that must be left untouched, and without any preconceived ideas about what the changes should be.

The way to evaluate the progress of improvement initiatives is to measure the effect of process improvements. The measures should be balanced among all of the key result areas, be communicated regularly, be easily understood, and be related to both operational and financial performance.

Two of the best measurements of process improvements are cycle time and the cost of quality. Cycle time is the total amount of time from the end of one output of a work process to the end of the next; cost of quality is the sum total of the cost of prevention, appraisal, and internal and external failures of the product to meet customer specifications. Cycle time is a good indicator of the operational impact of an improvement, and the cost of quality is a good measure of the overall financial impact of an improvement.

The importance of adequate measurement systems

When helping companies start the journey of continuous improvement, we often ask the leaders to brainstorm existing barriers to continuous performance improvement within the company. One important but seldom-mentioned barrier is inadequate measurement systems.

Manufacturing companies often cling to the traditional measures of efficiency and utilization of direct labor or equipment. Service organizations tend to measure very little except financial transactions, and health-care organizations suffer from the opposite extreme—they measure so much that little of the data is used as the basis for improvement.

The performance indicators used by any organization should meet the following three criteria:
1. they should be balanced among the key result areas,
2. they should continuously be updated and communicated to *all* employees, and
3. they should measure operational as well as financial performance.

Balanced indicators

Many organizations simply don't have a good picture of total performance because their set of key indicators is too narrow. To assure a balanced perspective, a company should have key indicators in each of the three key result areas discussed earlier (customer satisfaction, employee satisfaction, and positive financial and operational performance).

The organization should look to existing indicators. If measures are already in place that are familiar and frequently used, they are a good starting point. The number of measures should be limited to one or two for each of the key result areas. The greater the number of indicators, the greater the chance that activities will become scattered and the results diluted.

Continuously updated and shared

Ideally, all employees should have up-to-the-minute knowledge of their own performance on specific work processes and of the organization's performance as a whole. This may not always be possible, but all too often we see the other extreme: people are told very little, if anything, about total performance, and what little information does get communicated, such as last month's production figures, is too old to be of any real use.

Here are some guidelines for enabling key indicators to drive quality improvement:

1. Use graphs and charts rather than tables of numbers to communicate performance data.
2. Set a goal for communicating performance data to employees as close to real-time as possible. Some data, such as the results of employee or customer surveys, can cover the past year. Other data, such as changeover cycle time, should cover the past hour.
3. Make sure that middle managers and supervisors understand that one of the most important parts of their job is the communication of performance data.
4. Make certain that all people understand how their work can make an impact on these measurements.

Measuring operational as well as financial performance

We frequently find that companies rely on traditional cost-accounting numbers as a way to measure financial as well as operational performance. This has caused operations managers to take exactly the wrong steps to improve operations.

Deciding to increase inventories of components and finished products, planning long product runs with few changeovers, evaluating vendors on the basis of price alone, or ignoring the importance of orienting and training employees—these are all examples of poor decisions that can be the result of evaluating operational performance with cost-accounting numbers only.

Again, the two indicators that *should* be measured are process cycle times and the cost of quality. These measurements are important for two reasons.

They are customer-focused. They measure what customers care about. Customers don't care about direct labor or machine utilization rates, but they *do* care about how long it takes them to get the product and what shape it's in when they get it.

They have significant impact on overall costs. By focusing on the reduction of cycle times and minimizing the cost of quality, a company will maximize the impact of process improvements on operating cost.

Relationship of Cycle Time to Operating Cost

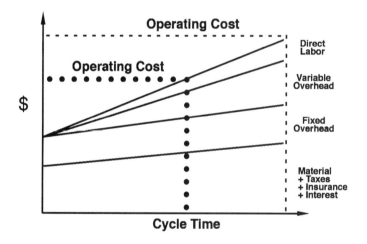

Cycle time

Cycle time is an important measurement and an extremely useful tool. Besides being a good measurement of specific process improvements, cycle time also serves as a valuable strategic tool because reducing cycle time is a highly productive way to improve customer satisfaction and to improve operating cost.

Measuring cycle times is also a very effective way to identify the greatest opportunities for improvement and to prioritize problem-solving. The use of cycle times as a tool for process improvement will be discussed in the chapter on time-based process improvement.

Cost of quality

The cost of quality is the sum total of the following costs:

Prevention. All costs associated with quality improvement activities, including workforce and systems development.

Appraisal. All costs associated with quality audits, testing, and inspections.

Internal failure. All costs associated with scrap and rework, including extra inventory.

External failure. All costs associated with warranty costs, liability exposure, customer ill-will, and loss of future sales.

Cost of Quality

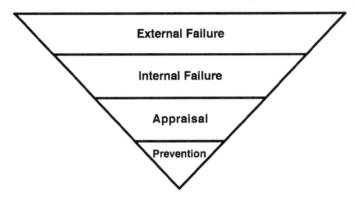

External Failure

Internal Failure

Appraisal

Prevention

Why measure the cost of quality

Careful attention to reducing the cost of quality can assure improvements in productivity, quality, and customer satisfaction, while at the same time reducing the cost of doing business.

The total cost of quality in a typical manufacturing company can be as much as 25% of manufacturing cost. In a service organization the figure can be as high as 40% of total revenues. Yet we have found that the cost of quality is uncharted territory in most organizations. We have seen the following happen repeatedly:

We'll say: "Think of any department in your organization and list two or three things that can go wrong: errors, defects, mistakes, variances, and so on. For each thing that can go wrong, describe the impact on the rest of the organization. What problems does it cause? What steps must be taken to correct the error? Finally, write down the total cost of these impacts."

Most people have no trouble until they get to the final question: the total cost. It's obvious that the total cost is considerable, but it's not something that's normally measured. It's easy to find out costs such as total wages and benefits, the cost of electricity for a month, or the cost of office supplies for the previous year. But it's very difficult to track the cost of doing things wrong. Because the cost of quality isn't usually measured, there typically is no activity focused on improving it.

While working with a hotel, we wanted to get a rough idea of the cost of poor quality in the restaurant. This hotel was very customer-focused, and on the rare occasion when a patron had a complaint about a meal, the tab was on the house, or comped in restaurant jargon. We asked one of the hotel's accountants for the total value of meals comped due to complaints in the past six months, expecting the answer to be available with a couple of computer keystrokes. Instead, the accountant led the way to a back hallway where cardboard boxes were stacked floor-to-ceiling. "These boxes," he said, "contain copies of bills for every customer who ate in the restaurant this year. Go through these boxes and look for the bills with a supervisor's signature on the back. They are the comped bills. When you pull them all out and add them up, you'll have the cost figure you're looking for."

How to measure it

Here are some tips that we have found to be helpful in managing the cost of quality.

Redistribute costs. The goal is not to reduce the cost of quality to zero, but to redistribute the cost so that more is spent on prevention and appraisal, and less on inspecting and correcting internal and external failures. As costs are redistributed, the more expensive internal and external failure costs will be reduced, resulting in an overall reduction in the total cost of quality.

Focus on processes. Companies will realize the most significant results by focusing on cross-functional business processes rather than on functions or small sub-processes.

Involve the people who perform the work. A company meets customer needs and expectations by involving its people, who gain satisfaction as they continuously improve the work processes which are designed to meet customer needs. Thus the loop is closed and the process continues.

Measure tangible and intangible costs. Cost systems should be designed to measure both the tangible (direct out-of-pocket) costs and the intangible (opportunity) costs of those processes with long cycle times and high variability.

Reward and recognize improvements. People should be rewarded, recognized, and promoted on the basis of reductions in process cycle times and the cost of quality. Far less emphasis should be placed on measures of activity and volume of production.

Some surprises at hand

There are often hidden costs in those changes and so-called improvements that are based strictly on price rather than on quality. Will a cost-reduction idea result in a true cost saving or in an additional quality cost? The answer to this question varies from project to project and from business to business.

For example, consider a manufacturer of parts stamped from sheet steel. To lower costs, this company decides to buy sheets of secondary steel rather than prime steel. What are the total costs of quality that need to be considered in this decision?

Quality costs exist in three of the four categories. There are appraisal costs, namely inspecting the sheets to sort out those with surface defects, and testing the hardness of each sheet. There are internal failure costs, namely scrap and rework which results from the inspection process. And there are external failure costs, namely the probability that some out-of-spec product may not be caught until it reaches the customer. In each quality cost area, it's necessary to identify the hidden costs. In this example, the cost of quality includes hidden costs such as the cost of sorting the good from the bad sheets and the cost of handling, rework, and disposition of the bad sheets.

Finally, when all these costs are considered and quantified, the question can be asked: is the difference between the cost of prime steel sheets and the cost of secondary steel sheets actually a cost saving?

Quality cost cannot be zero in any organization. The real issue is to define the pertinent quality costs for the company and its industry, and then to define how those costs can be used as a tool to evaluate changes and to gain market advantage.

High-performance workplaces do many things well. In particular, they do the basics well, and nothing is more basic than having and using good yardsticks to measure process improvements.

Suppose a football coach announces before a game that his team is taking the field without a game plan and that the coaching staff has not been involved in practices. The coach insists that the players are good and will figure out how to win. Would anyone bet on this team?

Nobody would. Yet every day many organizations attempt to compete without a game plan or a clear vision of where the organization is headed.

We have seen evidence of this when we have conducted assessments for various types of companies. As discussed in the first chapter, we often use the Malcolm Baldridge National Quality Award criteria because they are the most comprehensive in scope, because they include strategies that involve the entire organization in improving business processes, and because they emphasize results.

In these assessments, the lowest scores are consistently in three of the seven Baldridge categories: leadership; information and analysis; and strategic planning. The game plan, the playbook, and even the scorecard are often missing.

A word of warning

If little attention is given to these three categories, the following things may happen:
1. Quality can become the responsibility of a few people rather than that of everyone in the organization.
2. If not emphasized by top leadership, continuous improvement will become a low priority, something to do after everything else has been completed or when there is time—or never.
3. Improvement activities can become haphazard, with immediate problems receiving attention and long-term or difficult problems being ignored.
4. People may make improvements in their own work area or may concentrate on a pet project because it's the only one they have adequate information about. This kind of activity often has little impact on the performance of the organization as a whole.

A successful game plan

In team athletics, a successful coach creates game plans based on knowledge of his team's strengths and weaknesses, as well as those of the opponent. Players are confident of success because the coach has created a game plan based on accurate information. The game plan has been communicated so that all players know their roles and what is expected of them. Effective leadership has created a commitment by all team members to excellent performance in execution of the plan, and to winning.

Similarly, in a successful business, real-time information is used to create a performance improvement plan. The plan is understood by those who will be involved in its implementation, and it has their commitment. Leadership works to create a culture that facilitates the efforts of people to achieve the vision and goals.

Strategy or culture: which comes first?

Creating a high-performance organization requires a change in both strategy and culture. This is truly a daunting assignment. The tremendous difficulty of making this double change has led many to believe that it would be easier to change one first and then the other.

But where to start? Some experts believe the culture has to be changed first. This approach can result in initiatives that are long on awareness-raising and short on measured improvements. The alternative is to start with changes in strategy and measurable targets. But new strategies embedded in old cultures can create frustration and can fail to produce the desired results.

We have found that change in strategy will drive change in culture and that both must happen simultaneously. First, an organization develops specific targets and key indicators for improvement. Then, as part of the implementation plan, cultural barriers to those targets are identified and steps are taken to reduce or eliminate them.

Performance targets: an example

As an example of how strategy and culture are linked, consider the development of targets and indicators. In the culture of a traditional organization, a number of unfortunate circumstances surround the development of targets and indicators:

1. They are typically set by members of top management, who don't know the work situation as well as the people who actually perform the work.

2. Indicators usually have more to do with labor and equipment productivity than they do with customer satisfaction, cycle time, or the cost of quality.
3. They traditionally serve as demotivators. If a manager fails to meet a goal, bad things can happen. If a manager exceeds the goal, the targets are raised. The savvy manager just barely reaches the target, which holds back performance.

This is why Dr. Edwards Deming, world-renowned quality guru, said that targets and traditional cultures don't mix.

From a practical standpoint, we believe performance targets are necessary. They can provide focus and energy for improvement. If targets are put in the proper perspective, an organization can realize the benefits of establishing specific performance targets and key indicators without the unfavorable hammer-and-anvil effect discussed earlier.

How to do both

By setting specific targets, an organization achieves two ends: it creates energy for measurable performance improvements, and it drives the necessary cultural change. Here are some tips for developing a quality strategy that will create improvement in culture and performance:

The proper context. Senior leaders must establish a clear vision and a set of values that will serve as a frame of reference for all future activity. Once established, a quality culture must be created that supports the efforts and specific activities designed to achieve the vision. Quality improvement must be a key element of overall business plans; it cannot happen parallel to or outside these comprehensive strategies.

Outcome-oriented. Senior leaders should set broad goals with specific key indicators. These goals must be outcome-oriented rather than activity-oriented. For example: "Delivery performance will be 100%," not "We will install a bar-coding system to improve delivery performance." Goals are milestones along the road of improvement, not activities.

Deployment. Goals should be deployed throughout the organization so that managers, supervisors, and work groups can identify performance objectives aligned with those goals.

Alignment. Major systems, such as reward and recognition, should be aligned with the vision, values, goals, and objectives.

Tactics. Ideas for achieving these objectives should then be identified by the individuals or work groups who will develop actions plans for improvement.

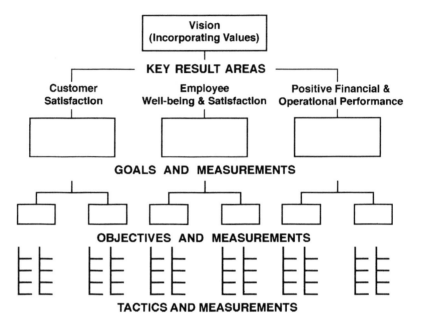

Communication. Key indicators need to be kept in front of all employees at all times. Everyone should be kept informed of progress toward the goals.

Momentum. An organization should plan for gradual change. Habits of a lifetime will not simply vanish. In the transition to a participative style of management, practice and experience will produce successes that will fuel the gradual transition.

Strategy is needed

Culture is difficult to change without a corresponding change in strategy, and new strategies are difficult to implement without a corresponding change in culture. Leadership should determine what needs to improve and how to measure it, should then identify the cultural barriers, and then should continuously work to reduce or eliminate them.

When leadership demonstrates commitment to the improvement strategy, others will follow suit. Effective leaders are personally involved in improvement activities. They talk about and promote the values and goals, and their day-to-day actions and decisions serve as a role model for the desired changes.

Implemented properly, performance improvement initiatives will provide good results and are well worth the effort. So why do so many companies stop short of achieving success? Because proper implementation is hard to do, and it takes a long time.

Successful implementation seems to necessitate one of quality's own basic themes: do it right the first time. If employees are frustrated by the first attempt, subsequent attempts will be infinitely more difficult.

By observing and coaching the implementation process in many companies, we have come to see the process as an evolution. When leadership recognizes the need to improve performance, leadership is committed to changed results rather than to the changes necessary to bring about the results. Ideally, leadership will also be convinced that it must change the way the business is run in order for the results to change. But leadership generally looks first to how its people do things and how other people need to change.

In the beginning stages, a willingness to support training and involvement of other people is often the maximum commitment that can be obtained from leaders. Experience has shown us that this is sufficient to get the process started. After preliminary efforts have produced tangible results, leadership will usually begin to make a more heartfelt commitment to changing the way the business is run.

Common pitfalls

Our experience with a wide variety of companies has also shown that successful implementation requires the avoidance of some common pitfalls. These pitfalls can be summed up in 12 frequently heard statements and beliefs that will very quickly sabotage any performance improvement initiative. Some of these will probably sound familiar.

1. *"I know some of our managers have reservations about involving all employees in the process of continuous improvement, but we can't let that slow down our plans for implementation. In time those managers will come around."*

Managers play a crucial role in the process. If they see themselves being left out of the loop and possibly out of a job, they are very likely to sabotage the process in subtle ways.

2. *"If the union doesn't want to get on board and support our efforts, we'll have to do it without them."*

Legally and practically, in a unionized setting, the only way to plan and implement the process is to do so with the full cooperation and involvement of union leaders and members.

3. *"It's our job as senior managers to develop the strategy. Once we have done that, we will present it to the steering committee and get them to buy in."*

Every effort needs to be made to get input and commitment from all people involved if they are to have any ownership in the strategy. Buy-in does not just happen.

4. *"The Human Resources Department should head up the implementation because they can determine what training is needed to get our employees motivated to make improvements."*

Implementation cannot be delegated to any one person or group. Line management throughout the organization must be involved.

5. *"There are only so many things I can personally be involved in. Just go ahead and do it!"*

Continuous improvement isn't something to *do*. It's a way of doing things. The process of leadership cannot be delegated, especially leadership for cultural change. Leadership can delegate anything but leadership itself.

6. *"The natural person to champion this effort is the Quality Assurance Manager. That's our quality expert."*

That's looking at quality with a small "q"—and what we are talking about is much bigger: organizational change and overall performance improvement, which includes not only quality assurance but also every work process in the company. This kind of quality can't be delegated to any one person or group. It needs to involve everyone.

7. *"We should begin by letting our suppliers know what we expect from them."*

This is buck-passing. The organization needs to clean up its own act first, and then begin to work with its suppliers.

8. *"The quicker we form teams and get everyone involved in improvement activities, the quicker we'll see some results."*

The reverse is probably true. Teams won't be effective and probably won't even survive without the support of the whole implementation process.

9. *"We don't need formal training. We're all intelligent people, and problem-solving is just common sense."*

That may be true in places where teams are firmly rooted in the culture, such as Japan. But our schools don't teach our children how to work in teams or how to solve problems logically. In general, we use the trial-

and-error method of problem-solving, and we place a premium on individual initiative.

10. *"The steering committee should approve all the problems the teams want to address. That will ensure that the teams are working on the right things and aren't just wasting time."*

This is naive. The steering committee represents the highest level of leadership. Its job is overall direction. Once the direction is clearly understood by everyone, the advantage of delegating problem-solving to the people who perform the work is that they know best what problems interfere with their ability to achieve maximum performance. They are also in the best position to develop effective solutions to those problems.

11. *"Our employees respond very well to our existing performance appraisal and incentive systems. We should make certain that our performance improvements don't interfere with those systems."*

Old systems may serve the old structure very well, but they probably won't serve the change process in their existing form. The organization needs to look at all systems and align them with the concepts of high performance. This is discussed in the chapters on deployment.

12. *"The pursuit of quality improvement is important, but we must keep in mind that the amount of product we ship determines the amount of our revenues."*

Not so. There are many intangible costs involved in focusing on quantity rather than on quality. What really determines the amount of revenues is the quantity of good product shipped, and what it costs to produce it.

An organization that espouses any of the beliefs in this dirty dozen is headed for serious difficulty in implementation. There may be obstacles at lower levels in the organization; we will discuss those obstacles later. But those obstacles can be overcome only if top leadership approaches implementation in the right way.

Fundamentals of implementation

There are some fundamental concepts that need to be understood in order to successfully implement performance improvement plans.

Senior leadership must take the lead. The first item of business is for senior leadership to take the time to discuss concerns and to reach consensus on all key pieces: the meaning of high performance, the need, the opportunity, the vision, the plan, the resources, the priority, the commitment, the support, and the personal changes that will need to be made to integrate the concepts of high performance on a day-to-day basis. In a unionized company, senior management must work together with union leadership from the very beginning and on through the entire process.

Goals and activities must be integrated. Every functional area or department, and ideally every individual, must be given an opportunity to provide input to the overall goals and objectives. Employees must also understand their department's role and their individual role in achieving these goals. Continuous improvement cannot succeed as a peripheral activity. It must be woven into the core of the way business is conducted on a daily basis.

Major systems must be aligned. All major systems must be aligned with the goals of the plan, especially the systems that reinforce performance, including performance appraisals, merit budgets, incentive and bonus plans, and recognition systems. Alignment of information and accounting systems is also very important.

What gets measured gets done. Specific and measurable goals and objectives are what will keep the activities on track. The feedback of measured results will provide momentum to sustain the activity. Measuring and focusing improvement on cycle time and on the cost of quality is the means by which an organization can realize the largest opportunities for internal cost reduction. This concept is discussed in detail in the chapters on measurement and on time-based process improvement.

Payback is proportional to commitment. The timing and magnitude of the results will be directly proportional to the resources dedicated. And the amount of resources dedicated will be perceived by everyone as the measure of priority and commitment.

Empowerment is essential. People are the true experts on their jobs. When people have the opportunity to have input in the day-to-day decision-making process and to take part in improvement activities, they are physically able to do a better job. Involvement creates ownership, which is the key to breakthrough improvements.

In short, successful empowerment is built on the foundation of three fundamental truths:

1. People are the true experts on their jobs and are best equipped to identify barriers and solutions.
2. More input results in better performance.
3. Ownership leads to commitment to any given course of action.

Implementation cannot be an experiment

Although continuous improvement involves a great deal of experimentation with systems and processes, it cannot be implemented as an experiment. Perhaps the most important key to successful implementation is the leadership's fervent and manifest belief that this approach is the *only* way for the business to survive and to thrive.

The following steps will help to maximize an organization's chances for successful implementation of its performance improvement plan:

1. collaboratively developing a workable plan;
2. taking the time to ensure the necessary ownership, alignment, support, and commitment to the plan by employees at all levels;
3. providing the resources necessary to execute the plan;
4. creating an environment that encourages involvement; and
5. understanding that once employees' expectations have been raised, there's no turning back.

Facilitation
1. Facilitator-Key Coordinator
2. Conflict Resolution

For an organization to successfully implement its performance improvement plan, and to support and sustain the plan over time, well-trained facilitators and a key coordinator are critical. The facilitators train and assist people in the tools used in group improvement activities. The key coordinator performs many roles, all of which revolve around keeping people and activities on track in pursuit of the goals.

It will take time and effort for performance improvement to become ingrained in an organization's way of doing business. Until that time, although it is the responsibility of top leadership, the organization needs someone whose top priority is to make it happen.

Toward this end, most organizations have found it necessary to identify and to train internal facilitators. By definition, a facilitator is someone who assists, who makes something easy or less difficult, or who helps to move a process forward.

Facilitator

The two primary requirements of a facilitator are first, to have a good working knowledge of the procedures, methods, and tools used in small-group improvement activities, and second, to have the ability to train and to assist others in the use of these skills. As more people get involved in improvement activities, the facilitator will also need to develop the skills necessary to resolve conflict and other interpersonal issues within groups and at interfaces throughout the organization.

A facilitator is not a group member. Although he—or she—may lead a discussion in terms of keeping it on track, the facilitator does not take part in the content of the discussion. The facilitator's role is in the process, *not* in the content.

Key coordinator

In the implementation of a performance improvement initiative, companies need to identify and train someone to coordinate the effort throughout the organization. We refer to this role as the key coordinator. He must serve as the change agent, corporate conscience, sounding board, trainer, liaison, and, most important, facilitator of group activities at all levels of the organization. In short, the key coordinator is the person who keeps people and activities on track.

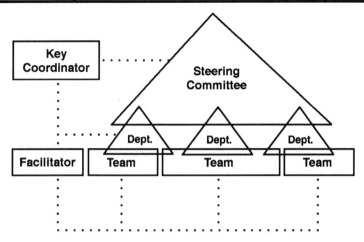

The many roles of the key coordinator can be condensed into five major categories: facilitator, champion, change agent, liaison, and internal consultant. In these roles, the key coordinator devotes attention to organizational systems, to goals, to procedures, to roles, and to interpersonal relationships. The responsibilities involved in each of these roles are as follows.

Facilitator. In this role, the key coordinator ensures that the work of performance-improvement teams is consistent with the company's long-range improvement plans. He also helps work groups and individuals understand their role in the pursuit of the company's goals, as well as what support and involvement they need to give to assist others with their improvement efforts.

Champion. To champion the pursuit of high performance, the key coordinator must understand the values and be proficient in the tools and techniques of performance improvement. He must be knowledgeable of the company's specific performance-improvement plan, and able to pass along that knowledge through training. He must keep current with the latest strategies by reading, attending seminars, and participating in networking groups. It's important that the key coordinator be a role model of the values and behavior that are expected of everyone, and that he strive to keep performance improvement uppermost in the minds of people at all levels in the organization. Finally, the key coordinator must continually try to work himself out of a job, as leadership begins to take on more and more of these responsibilities.

Change agent. In this role the key coordinator stimulates creative thinking. He encourages risk-taking and innovation by working to create a blame-free environment that permits people to fail as long as they learn from it. He challenges complacency and paradigms, encouraging people to break self-imposed restrictions that stand in the way of success. He anticipates barriers, serves as a troubleshooter, and works to create an environment that allows employee involvement to succeed. He also needs to develop a skill known as influencing. Influencing skills are vital, because the key coordinator typically has very little legitimate power. If he has the support of senior management, he has referred power, which means that people will think of senior management when they see him. However, the key coordinator's ability to succeed in implementing the necessary changes and in getting things done on a day-to-day basis will depend in large measure on how well he can develop his influencing skills.

Liaison. In this area of responsibility, the key coordinator facilitates effective communication at all levels and interfaces. He sees that every team or group has a charter that clearly identifies all relevant details, including its purpose and how it will know that it has successfully completed its mission. He also keeps records.

Internal consultant. Here the key coordinator develops resources; ideally, he clones himself. He is a trainer of groups, and he makes sure each group is equipped with the right tools for its job. Finally, he is a sounding board, fielding questions and continually attempting to allay skepticism and fears relative to the change process.

No single model

There is no single path to perfection as a key coordinator. Exactly what the key coordinator does and how he does it will vary according to the values of his organization, the nature of the industry, and his personal background and style.

Consider, for instance, these two examples from our *Profiles*: Dr. Donald Plante, Vice President, Quality and Technology, at Picker International; and Dave Udovich, Vice President, Product Technology and Quality Assurance, at Van Dorn Demag. Although both individuals are in manufacturing companies and come from technical backgrounds, they perform the key coordinator role in very different ways. Each, as you will note in the *Profiles*, has one very important trait in common. That trait is success.

CONFLICT RESOLUTION

Conflict is a fact of life in every organization. Although conflict is commonly viewed in a negative light, as something that results in winners and losers, conflict *can*—if managed properly—produce positive results.

Win-win solutions are the key to positive results. It takes considerable time and effort to achieve a win-win solution, but the alternatives are far more costly and time-consuming. Unresolved, repressed, or ignored conflict merely goes underground and resurfaces to consume time and energy that is better spent on developing new ways to improve performance. For this reason, the key coordinator and others who serve as facilitators need to be skilled in win-win conflict resolution.

Dealing with conflict

Conflict occurs in many ways and in many places: between departments, between line and staff personnel, between different levels of the organization, between unions and management, among team members, and between individuals.

When we ask people what they think about conflict, we get responses like "emotional" or "destructive" or "not acceptable." Conflict is seen as a fight that produces a winner and a loser, and usually results in bad feelings.

Most people have a preferred method of dealing with conflict. Some of the more common methods are:
1. Bottle it up.
2. Ignore it and hope it goes away.
3. Squelch it with an iron fist.

All these methods have negative results, but there is another way that has positive results:
4. Explore all sides of the issue to find underlying interests and a solution that will satisfy the interests of the parties involved.

Handled in this way, conflict can actually improve the working relationship among people.

Win-Win Conflict Resolution, also known as Alternate Dispute Resolution or Interest-Based Conflict Resolution, is a matter of building consensus around a chosen alternative in order to resolve a dispute. As will be discussed in the chapter on effective teams, conflict resolution skills must be mastered by teams if they are to become truly effective.

Win-Win Conflict Resolution involves the exploration of alternatives to find one that will satisfy the interests and needs of the parties involved. This process works because people's needs and interests tend to be much broader and less conflicting than do the initial positions taken. Using the win-win method, each person presents his or her interests and needs, and listens as everyone else does likewise. The group then seeks areas of agreement rather than debating areas of disagreement.

The following is a very simple example that's used to demonstrate this method. Two children are fighting over an orange. One child says, "I saw it first," (an attempt to resolve the conflict by claiming rights). The other says, "So what! I'm bigger than you are" (the use of power). They argue; they may fight physically. One wins and gets the orange, and the other loses and goes away angry. Win-lose was inevitable.

Suppose instead that someone—a facilitator—were to ask each child, "Why do you want the orange?" The first child might say, "I'm hungry, and I like oranges." The second might say, "I need the seeds for a science project at school." Each child has interests which can be met so that both children can get what they want.

A real-life example

Of course, real life is usually much more complex. The following is an example that surfaced with one of our clients in the course of a steering committee's planning retreat.

Union and management representatives had just agreed to pursue the implementation of self-directed work teams. Having agreed to this concept, the union representative pointed out that in his work area the first-shift supervisor was going to retire soon. He suggested that the second-shift supervisor be switched to first shift because the second-shift employees were more senior and thus good candidates for self-direction.

The production manager took the position that a new supervisor should be hired to fill the first-shift vacancy. The union representative became adamant and changed his suggestion to a demand that the second-shift supervisor be switched. It soon became apparent that if left to continue, this conflict would escalate to a dispute that would undermine the spirit of the retreat.

Using the concepts of win-win conflict resolution, we asked them to explore the interests behind the positions they had taken. The union representative's interest was to have the first self-directed team created in his own area and on his shift, the second shift, so that he could experience first-hand how it worked. He assumed that management would not want to put the first team on his shift if that shift had a supervisor.

The production manager's interest was to make a smooth transition to self-direction, which he knew would require someone to perform the new role of facilitator, trainer, liaison, and coordinator. He assumed that this role in the new work system would be filled by the former supervisors.

The resolution was to hire someone specifically for the new role, to place that person on the second shift, and to create the first self-directed team on that shift as well. Both interests were satisfied, and the conflict was resolved in win-win fashion.

Steps to better resolutions of conflict

Facilitators can help people become better at managing conflict by:
1. Encouraging acknowledgment that conflict exists. Conflict can be resolved only if it's out in the open.
2. Attempting to defuse feelings raised during the dispute. This can be done by facilitating a discussion in which each party gets to speak without interruption, or by having the parties write about the dispute before any discussion takes place.
3. Encouraging each party to understand the underlying interests of the others. By having people ask, "Why do you want this? What do you want to achieve?" the facilitator helps individuals get beyond the positions they are taking to an understanding of the underlying reasons.
4. Helping the parties to see areas where they agree rather than concentrating on areas of disagreement. It's productive to build on areas of agreement because many disputes actually involve only a few areas of disagreement and many areas of agreement.
5. Encouraging discussion of creative, alternative solutions that meet everyone's needs, and then using consensus to reach agreement on one approach to resolve the conflict.

Conflict is inevitable in any organization, but the energy of conflict can become a productive force by using win-win techniques. People will grow, teams will mature, communication will improve, and the organization will benefit.

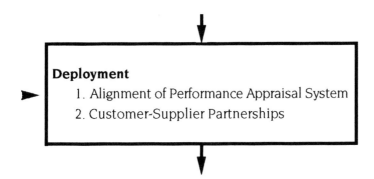

Deployment
    1. Alignment of Performance Appraisal System
    2. Customer-Supplier Partnerships

If a performance improvement plan is to succeed in accomplishing its goals, everyone in the organization needs to understand the vision and values, be aware of the goals, give thought to their personal role in support of the plan, and commit to measurable objectives for improvement in their own work areas. Moreover, everyone must be willing to suggest ideas or tactics for improvement and to participate in developing those tactics. This is what we refer to as deployment.

As part of deployment, all major systems should be aligned with the company's improvement strategy. Of these systems, perhaps the most important is performance appraisal and review. The way an appraisal is conducted and the behaviors it assesses are high-profile examples of a company's real priorities. Unfortunately, many companies proceed without incorporating their vision, goals, and objectives into the performance appraisal system. All too often, these systems address individual performance and the more traditional controls and measurements.

Like all other systems in the organization, a performance appraisal system can and should actively support the pursuit of high performance. Leaders need to motivate, inspire, and set a positive example of the behavior expected of other people.

Many of us have seen the negative side of performance appraisal systems that are poorly constructed, poorly conducted, or both. Such systems can result in anger and turmoil rather than customer focus and employee commitment. Moreover, they fail to support the goals of the organization.

Appraisal systems can be constructed and implemented so as to support the company's values and goals. When an organization embarks on the journey of continuous improvement, it's important to review the performance appraisal system and to revise it to reinforce the concepts of high-performance work systems. Even more important, these systems should reinforce a leadership style that will allow the concepts to succeed.

Three basic steps are involved in the transformation of a traditional performance appraisal system to one that reinforces the values and supports the vision and goals.

Analyze performance criteria

The first step is to decide what activities support the plan and what performance is important to evaluate. Where is the company going? How will the company get there? The answers to these questions highlight which aspects of performance are truly important.

Does top management expect more collaboration and teamwork? Does it desire more involvement by employees? Is performance satisfactory if it equals that of the previous year, or is continuous improvement expected? The desired behaviors and results need to be praised and encouraged in the course of the job and reinforced in the course of the performance review.

Review and revise the current system

The second step is to review what the existing appraisal system measures and what it ignores—in effect, what behavior it reinforces:

1. Does the system appraise traits or specific criteria of job performance?
2. What behaviors do the criteria actually encourage?
3. Do the criteria encourage behaviors related to high performance, such as teamwork, customer focus, and continuous improvement?
4. Does the system function merely as a report card, or do employees play an active role in setting objectives for improvement?
5. Does the system assign blame, or does it encourage risk-taking?

It's important to develop an appraisal that clearly asks for performance information about behavior that supports the organization's values and goals. Consider who should provide input for revising the system. We recommend that leadership seek input from many people at all levels and across all functions. It's also important to allow for ongoing suggestions for future improvement.

If the current system is found to be drastically inadequate for measuring and reinforcing teamwork, customer focus, and the other elements of a high-performance organization, then it will probably be easier to draft a completely new system rather than to revise the old one.

Train and communicate

The third step is to provide thorough training for those people responsible for appraising, usually supervisors and managers. Training should include basic appraisal skills as well as the specifics of the new appraisal system. To work well, a system depends on skilled appraisers who are confident in that role.

Employees need to receive detailed information about the new process. As with any change effort, good communication reduces resistance and promotes understanding and cooperation.

When an organization aligns its appraisal system with its values, it sends a clear message that it expects those values to be incorporated into daily work. The performance appraisal is too powerful a tool to be ignored when implementing a long-range plan for performance improvement.

Partnering offers many powerful benefits both for customers and for suppliers. This concept is relatively new. In the not-so-distant past, companies would send out word to their suppliers that they would have to cut their prices by x% per year for the next 5 years. Suppliers would grit their teeth, analyze margins, look for corners to cut, and wonder if it was worth it or even possible to stay in business.

Some customers viewed the ideal as having lots of suppliers and making them compete to keep them on their toes. However, that philosophy can backfire. Placed in such a situation, suppliers may cut quality as well as cost. It's important to look at the total cost—not just the quoted price.

Talking with the purchasing agents of several large corporations, we have found that they no longer look for traditional responses to cost cutting. What they do want is suppliers who run an efficient operation with consistently good quality, on-time delivery, and outstanding service. Ultimately, companies want to partner with their suppliers for mutual benefit and profit. In this way, customers help develop their suppliers.

Almost all organizations function in both the customer and the supplier mode. Let's look at the subject from both sides.

Customer strategies

Customers need to reduce their supplier base so that they have a manageable number of qualified suppliers. Customers can then make suppliers part of the continuous improvement process and can develop mutually beneficial partnerships.

How much opportunity for improvement do suppliers represent? In manufacturing, material cost is usually at least 50% of the total manufacturing cost. Thus the development of suppliers and the alignment of suppliers with the company's internal improvement process represents at least 50% of a company's opportunities for improvement.

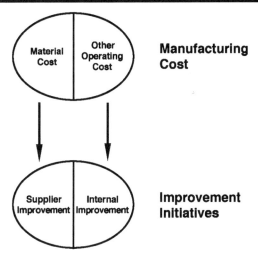

Selecting purchases to certify

One way to ensure satisfaction while reducing cost is to implement a system of supplier certification, which assures that suppliers meet specific standards of quality, delivery, and service. The first step is to determine which purchases merit attention. These purchases fall into several types:

1. those that account for the largest dollar volume,
2. those that provide major value-added elements to the product,
3. those that must meet key specifications, or
4. those that cause an inordinate amount of trouble.

By focusing on these purchases, a company will maximize its return on the investment in its supplier certification system.

Choosing suppliers with whom to partner

The next step is to evaluate the suppliers of these purchases and to select the one or two suppliers most capable of meeting all requirements. Cost, quality, delivery, and customer-service information should be tracked. The selection of suppliers should be based on data of each supplier's performance and should be collected over at least a one-year period.

This evaluation will identify the top suppliers for each item. By reducing the supplier base, a company gains the opportunity to develop a productive relationship with each supplier.

Monitoring supplier performance

The next step is to determine that each supplier selected is indeed capable of meeting the requirements on a consistent basis. Large corporations use periodic quality audits to determine the capability of their suppliers' quality systems. For small companies, however, this method can represent a huge investment of time and money. Having a third party conduct supplier audits is an effective and cost-efficient alternative.

The performance of suppliers should be monitored constantly. Should problems be spotted, the company should notify the supplier, describe the problem, request action, and be ready and willing to help. When a supplier consistently meets or exceeds requirements, the costs can be reduced by eliminating incoming inspection of shipments from that supplier.

Teams for mutual advantage

Forming teams that include suppliers and customers can be advantageous in a number of ways. Such teams typically speed up the problem-solving process by involving the people who are closest to the issues. The supplier discovers the real needs of the customer, sometimes for the first time, and can then direct energies to the most important problems.

Through this process, suppliers can become part of the business family, able to share the customer's triumphs and to support the customer through difficult times. However, this will happen only if the customer is willing to reciprocate.

An example

One example of a customer-supplier team that achieved outstanding results was an outgrowth of a quality problem that an automotive stamping plant experienced with coils of steel provided by one of its steel suppliers. In spite of several efforts to correct the problem through traditional means, rejects continued to grow to the point that 30% of all coils received by the stamping plant were rejected due to some form of damage.

As a result, the customer-supplier relationship deteriorated to the point that pictures of the coils were being taken by the supplier as the steel was loaded, and by the customer as it was unloaded, to assist with the process of placing blame. At this point the trucking company also became involved in the arguments.

When all other attempts to solve this problem seemed to have failed, a joint customer-supplier team was formed to address the issue. The team was comprised of shop-floor workers at the steel plant which processed and shipped the coils, together with the workers who received and used the steel at the stamping plant.

After training, the team met once a month for about eight hours. The results were dramatic. The steel plant had previously focused all its energy on ensuring that the sidewalls of the coils were perfectly straight, assuming that uneven winding was causing the damage. However, the stamping plant was not at all concerned about the sidewalls; it *was* concerned about the damage caused by loose inner and outer wraps. The steel plant, assuming that the customer did not use these wraps, had taken very little care to protect them.

The solution, an outgrowth of the change in focus and the direct communication between workers at the two sites, reduced the rejects from 30% to 0%. Now, when a coil problem crops up, a team member from the stamping plant makes a direct phone call to a team member from the steel supplier so the problem can be corrected before formal rejections are required. The savings to both the customer and the supplier have been enormous. Equally important, the relationship that has developed has generated untold benefits in terms of future business between these two companies.

Initiating partnerships with customers

In the supplier role, a company can also take the initiative to develop a customer-supplier partnership. The supplier can:
1. Understand what it takes to run an efficient, quality-oriented operation.
2. Implement a process which will involve employees in finding more efficient ways to operate.
3. Involve employees in a demonstration project that yields quick results and a payoff that can be used to help defray the costs of implementing a plant-wide improvement process.
4. Once these activities are in place, invite customers to visit the supplier's site. This will begin to establish a more personal relationship and will enable customers to see the supplier's efforts

and results first-hand. Customers may be able to offer some valuable advice. Some larger customers also provide training in quality-improvement tools and techniques. From our experience, direct contact between customers and their suppliers' employees almost always produces mutual benefits.

5. Suppliers can partner with customers and let customers know how they might help reduce supplier costs and thus prices. This process worked so well for one of our clients that their largest customer made our client an integral part of their expansion plans and significantly increased orders, on the condition that our client continue with improvement initiatives.

Tips for partnering with customers

Customer-supplier relationships typically result in money-saving ideas such as blanket purchase orders, the specification of readily available raw materials, and supplier involvement in the design of new products. As partnerships are developed between customers and suppliers, mutual trust will also develop.

For example, a purchasing director asked suppliers to inform him of increases in externally imposed overhead. Thus, when Medicare and Worker's Compensation premiums were increased, the purchasing director was prepared to accept higher prices to compensate for those increased costs.

These are just two examples of how customer-supplier partnerships can be developed, and of the tremendous potential benefits they can create.

Continuous Improvement Initiatives
1. ISO and QS 9000
2. Creative Problem-solving
3. TIme-based Process Improvement
4. Effective Teams
5. Empowerment

Once the performance improvement plan has been communicated and deployed, the leadership group needs to set priorities and charter improvement activities. This involves forming teams, clarifying the levels of their empowerment, defining their mission, and training them in the proper tools for the task at hand. In addition, the continued success of teams will require good facilitation, receptivity to their recommendations, and recognition of their successes.

ISO AND QS 9000

The focus of ISO 9000, the international quality standard, is narrower and more basic than the Baldridge criteria. ISO can be pursued for different reasons and on different levels. Some people view it as simply a marketing tool, while others see it as a means of achieving significant quality improvement. Some see it as simply a quality system certification, while others see it as a basic operating system.

If a company's customers require ISO certification, and if that company doesn't already have a quality system in place, ISO 9000 is an excellent place to start its continuous improvement initiatives. It's important to keep in mind that ISO is only one part of an organization's efforts to achieve high performance.

By now most businesses are familiar with both ISO 9000 and QS 9000, the related standard in the American automotive industry. ISO and QS 9000 are basic management systems designed to assure customers that a supplier's processes meet a specified level of excellence.

In short, these standards require three things of any company:
1. to say what it does,
2. to do what it says it does, and
3. to prove it to the satisfaction of an accredited third-party certifying agency known as a registrar.

The driving force that developed ISO 9000 was the concept of standardization of quality system requirements. Although most of us agree with this concept in the abstract, there have been problems with several aspects of developing the standard and with how to apply that standard to specific industries and to specific companies. Ultimately, we feel that the global marketplace will have some sort of universally recognized quality certification or standard, but no one can say exactly what it will be. It may be ISO, it may be a derivative, or it may be an entirely different standards.

In today's marketplace, if a company's customers require certification to ISO or QS 9000 standards, the decision is clear-cut. If, on the other hand, customers show little interest in it, a company has much more latitude regarding if and how to use the standard.

Much is left to the company to decide

Some people have criticized ISO for requiring an inordinate amount of documentation, but in fact neither ISO nor QS 9000 requires any specific amount of documentation, and neither one specifies the type or format to be used.

For example, ISO specifically requires the company to have procedures for contract review and for handling changes in contracts. This implies a minimum of two procedures, one for each of these two processes. It's up to the individual company to determine how it develops the procedures for the contract review process, the number of procedures, their format, and how documentation is controlled.

Value-added activity

In the ISO standard, documentation is described as "a dynamic, value-adding activity." Few people disagree with the idea that a business should put its important operating procedures in writing and keep them up to date. That's just good business practice. Typically, however, it's hard to find the time to do this consistently.

What our clients are finding as they comply with ISO requirements is that by agreeing to the content of a procedure and following it consistently, fewer errors are made, less time is spent correcting what errors do occur, and inefficiencies are discovered. Furthermore, continuous improvement is almost impossible to achieve without first knowing the current methodology and procedures. When an improvement activity or project is begun, it is first necessary to describe the current methodology.

ISO and QS 9000 prescribe a system whereby a company maintains information, including changes, on a continuous basis. This system has the added benefit of substantially increasing the visibility of the impact of improvements.

Tribal knowledge, procedural drift

Everyone has experienced the situation in which someone performs a procedure that is unfamiliar. Quite often this situation results in errors, misinformation, scrap, rework, or, worst of all, an unhappy customer.

When procedures are not documented and work is done through tribal knowledge, procedures tend to drift in an uncontrolled manner until what is being done only slightly resembles the original intent.

The secret to success in implementation of ISO is to decide what documentation is needed in order to control the consistency of the work processes and then to check the ISO requirements to see whether everything has been covered.

This doesn't have to be done by someone intimately familiar with ISO compliance. Nor does it need a skilled writer. It does require someone who can convey information quickly and efficiently, in a systematic, orderly, and understandable manner.

The person who performs a work procedure is the one who should write it down. Then a team of people connected with the procedure should examine it for completeness and compatibility with other procedures. Only then should the focus move to compliance with ISO requirements.

Controlling the cost of quality

An interesting aspect of ISO is that it addresses all the areas of quality costs. It indirectly encourages companies to identify and document not only the four basic quality costs—appraisal, prevention, internal failure, and external failure—but the other hidden costs as well.

For example, the standard requires that nonconforming material be clearly identified and isolated until its disposition can be determined. This is an excellent opportunity to identify how much time and money are spent on rejects or scrap.

The standard also allows for incoming material to be released prior to verification for urgent production purposes as long as a system is in place to trace and locate product used from that material. This again is an excellent opportunity to identify the total cost of inferior material introduced into the process. The standard doesn't address the analysis or control of these costs. That's up to the individual company.

Quality costs can never be zero in today's business world. At a very minimum there will be the cost of some system of quality assurance. Companies must identify these costs and control them. Therefore, it is imperative that all businesses develop or strengthen the system which directly controls the quality of their product or service. ISO may be a good model for accomplishing this.

When it becomes necessary to change the way things are done, the same process should be followed. This is not what usually happens. It's all too easy to omit the drudgery of following through and documenting the change. This inertia must be overcome in order to maintain ISO certification. The very fact that change must be documented is one of the benefits of formal third-party certification which entails periodic surveillance audits.

ISO or QS 9000 certification is not a necessity for every company, but the basic tenets of the standard are the essential foundation of any high-performing organization.

U.S. industry historically has made problem-solving the province of the manager responsible for the area concerned. The manager decided what problems were most important, what solutions would be tried, and when. These solutions were developed without any input from the people who worked directly with the problems, or with input that was greatly distorted as it made its way upward through the organization. To seek input from nonmanagement people was unheard of.

Managers often feared that problems would be seen as a sign of their incompetence, so the importance or even the existence of a problem was often denied, with the result that a multitude of opportunities for improvement were missed.

The responses to suggestions are familiar and notorious: "We tried that once," or "We already discussed that," or "That would never work here." The only problem acceptable to managers was poor implementation, which could be blamed on someone else. Changes were considered only as a last resort, because a change was an admission that the original decision was not a good one.

The legacy of this madness is the persistence of problems that could have been solved years ago.

On a journey of continuous improvement, it should be understood that whatever we decide today and whatever works well today can probably be replaced by a better idea at some point in the future.

It is also a given that we need to use all of our resources, the most important of which is our people. No one person can be expected to have all the answers. It is not a sign of weakness to seek or accept input from others, and groups are far more successful than individuals when it comes to developing simple, inexpensive, and effective solutions to creative problems.

Divergent and convergent thinking

Problem-solving is comprised of two types of thinking: divergent and convergent. Divergent thinking is creative thought development, and its goal is to produce many different ideas; it expands thoughts from one idea to many different but related ideas. Convergent thinking is rational, and its goal is to reach a decision, to select one from the many ideas created in the divergent thought process.

The human brain cannot effectively perform these two functions simultaneously. Divergent thinking, by its nature, must be done in the absence of logic and judgment. Convergent thinking, on the other hand, must be done in the presence of logic and judgment.

It is difficult to abandon logic and judgment, even for a short period of time. Brainstorming is the tool that is used to help defer the use of logic and judgment and to isolate the divergent thought process.

The rules of brainstorming are easy to understand: record all ideas, don't use logic or judgment, don't criticize, don't discuss ideas, aim for quantity, and so on. The trick is to stick to the rules; all too often, the group allows logic and judgment to creep into the brainstorming activity.

The tendency is to evaluate ideas as they come up, thinking of all the reasons why something may not work. This is like driving with the brakes on. A group that is brainstorming effectively can come up with 70-100 ideas in just four or five minutes.

If the group attempts to do both thought processes simultaneously, however, members may start to discuss and debate one of the first few ideas, and that may be as far as the group gets in the development of new and different ideas. The usual excuse is, "We got all the good ideas right away." The truth is that most of the more creative ideas come up later in the process.

A useful technique in problem-solving is to state the ruling paradigms—those limitations that have always been present, the way things always have been done. If a group begins by articulating its paradigms, the group can become truly creative, by using the tool of brainstorming to find alternatives outside those paradigms.

The problem-solving process

Most problem-solving processes are very similar. The explicit number of steps may vary, but the elements are the same, and divergent and convergent thinking are used alternately throughout the process. We use the following six-step process:

1. Identify the problem. (Brainstorm; reach consensus).
2. Define the problem. (What do team members see happening? Why is it important?)
3. Analyze the causes. (List and categorize the possible causes; collect and analyze data; determine the root, or most significant, causes.)
4. Develop alternative solutions. (Brainstorm; evaluate alternatives.)

5. Choose a best solution. (Reach consensus; describe the solution in detail; list the costs and benefits.)
6. Develop an action plan. (Make a step-by-step list of instructions; identify who will do what and by when; identify the resources needed.)

Defining the problem

We have found that people generally have a lot of difficulty separating effects, causes, and solutions. The difficulty stems from the broad use of the word "problem" to mean all three things. The group's first task is to sort out these three things so that the group can develop a problem statement, or definition, that isolates the effect from the causes and the solutions.

It's very important to state the problem in neutral terms, without any predetermined thoughts about causes or solutions. If this isn't done, the process won't work. If a team gets stalled at any point, it should go back and analyze its statement of the problem.

Here's an example. A team stated as its problem, "There is a lack of forklift service at the exit end of the production line." When the team got to the fourth step of the problem-solving process, it was unable to develop alternative solutions. The team had only one solution, which was inevitable: provide more forklifts at the exit end of the production line. If a problem is stated as being a lack of something, then of course the only solution is for that something to be present.

To overcome this dilemma, we asked the team members to go back to the beginning and state what they saw happening. Completed parts were put in a big metal container, and when it was full, people had to wait for a forklift to remove this heavy container and replace it with an empty one. This is a very different problem: inability to move full containers in a timely way. When the group went through the steps again, it came up with the solution of putting casters on the bottoms of the containers so they could be moved out by hand, even when full.

The team discovered that one of the root causes of the problem was forklift traffic and congestion and that *fewer* forklifts were needed, the opposite of what the team had initially thought. Adding another forklift would only have made the problem worse.

Analyzing possible causes

A basic and useful tool for analyzing possible causes of a problem is the cause-and-effect diagram, also called an Ishikawa or fishbone diagram. The same rules apply as in brainstorming, but ideas are put in categories:

* man, or human error in the system;
* method, or flaws in the process;
* machine, or the equipment used;
* material, or anything that is consumed, including information;
* environment, or everything else beyond the team's control; and
* any further categories the group wants to add.

Group members must effectively overcome group-think, or the feeling that the group can determine causes without research. The actual causes of the problem are found through careful collection and analysis of information. Root causes cannot be identified by making assumptions, by voting, or by consensus.

Team members must investigate and gather data. The leader organizes a data search for every item on the fishbone, and this search is outlined in an analysis chart that identifies who will track down what data and by when. This chart becomes the agenda for future meetings. The chart also helps the group recall the data collected and reviewed at earlier meetings.

When the team has researched all the items, it must sort out the significant few root causes from this mountain of data. The important thing is to avoid solving one of the trivial many causes. According to the Pareto Principle, 80% of the problem can be traced to 20% of the causes.

If the group is dealing with quantitative data, this is a point where some of the tools of statistical process control may be useful in determining the root cause.

For qualitative data, root-cause analysis is a useful tool. This tool requires asking at least five times why the effect, or symptom, has occurred. This tool prevents the team from ending its investigation prematurely. Each successive answer forces a deeper analysis of the cause until the group has identified the root cause, or the cause that is responsible for the majority of the problem.

Generating possible solutions

After the root cause has been identified, the team is ready to generate possible solutions. After members have brainstormed a number of alternatives, they again move into a data-collecting stage. They need to evaluate alternative solutions, to conduct trials, to consult experts, and to weigh the costs and benefits.

Choosing a best solution by consensus

There are many ways to make decisions. We strongly suggest consensus, especially at this point. Creative problems, by their very nature, have more than one solution that will work. How well a solution will work depends on the support for that solution by the people who will implement it. Consensus creates ownership and builds support.

Consensus is agreement based on a thorough discussion of all of the relevant facts. It is not reached by voting, averaging, persuading, bartering, giving in, or compromising. It is reached by exploring many alternatives until one is found that everyone in the group can live with and support.

All members need to share their knowledge and experience in a rational manner, to listen to all opinions in a logical and thoughtful way, and to explore alternatives and evaluate them on the basis of agreed-upon criteria.

Decisions by consensus are difficult to attain, and they almost always take more time than decisions made by other means. But for lasting solutions to creative problems, it is consensus that builds the support that will ensure the success of any given solution.

Troubleshooting

Troubleshooting requires the team to continually ask certain questions. Whose interests will be affected by this decision? If this were done, what could go wrong? Questions such as these really bring out the organizational politics. Because the answers will identify aspects of the problem that may have a tangential impact on people outside the team, it's necessary to troubleshoot throughout the problem-solving process.

At this point, the people identified by the troubleshooting should be brought into the group in order to get their input during the decisionmaking process, or sooner if possible. The only way to ensure people's support is to include them in the decision.

A team usually needs to convince and get approval of someone outside the group that its recommendations should be implemented. That person may also have an opinion about what the solution should be. If the team, in its presentation, explains that it evaluated that alternative and gives a good reason for discarding it, the team has a better chance of having its solution approved. Otherwise, there is a danger that the team will be told it hasn't been thorough enough and that it needs to go back and rethink its solution.

All things considered, the team's solution is usually the best: it will work best because the team owns it and will make sure that it works.

Developing an action plan

At this stage, the team develops another chart on which it records the following: detailed action steps, individuals with responsibility for carrying out the action steps, and deadlines for completion of the action steps. Carrying out an action plan is like assembling a bicycle on Christmas Eve: when the job is done, no parts are left over and the solution is implemented as intended. If the plan isn't developed in sufficient detail, there's often considerable margin for error.

When individuals, work groups, or teams are chartered to improve a work process, they face a wide variety of opportunities for improvement. The challenge is how to get the maximum improvement possible with the minimum investment of time and expense. The answer is to focus on reducing the cycle time, which is the amount of time it takes to perform the work process in question. More precisely, cycle time is the total elapsed time between successive outputs of any given work process.

Where to start?

Every process has several variables that can be measured. Those most commonly analyzed are output quantity, productivity, quality, cost, waste, and cycle time. To the team whose mission it is to improve a process, it becomes obvious that the ideal improvement will increase output, productivity, and quality at the same time that it decreases cost, waste, and cycle time.

We have seen time and again that this mountain of opportunity provides so many options that it's easy to get confused when deciding where to start. Concentrating the improvement efforts on the reduction of cycle time will focus efforts quickly and easily on the greatest opportunity for improvement.

The problem with other approaches

A surprisingly common approach is to select one of the variables more or less at random. This quickly solves the problem of where to start, but runs a very high risk of getting a relatively small return on the improvement efforts. A lot of time may be spent addressing one of the many trivial opportunities for improvement rather than focusing on one of the significant few opportunities that will yield major results. Moreover, because all of the variables are interrelated, it is possible to improve quality but reduce productivity or to improve productivity but increase cost.

Another approach, which would appear to be more methodical, is to focus on cost. The difficulty with this approach is one of measurement. Seldom is cost information known or available in the detail necessary to match up with a step-by-step analysis of a work process. The figures that are available are often allocations or standards rather than actual costs.

Yet another method is the lean manufacturing approach. In this method, inventory is lowered in order to highlight problems and to force their solution. If not done carefully, this can be a very costly and needlessly painful experience.

The solution: measure cycle time

Measuring cycle time makes it possible to identify the greatest opportunities for improvement simply by analyzing what takes the most time. The steps are presented below, using the framework of our time-based process-improvement model.

Define objectives. Because the actual value-added or required time of any work process is such a small percent of the total, most cycle times can be reduced by at least 50% without making any significant investment in new tools or equipment.

Observe and map the existing process. This step involves observing the existing process from beginning to end and then mapping it, or creating a flow diagram. This can best be done by a cross-functional team that has representatives from all of the work functions performed in the process.

Collect time data. It's normally a fairly simple task to measure the amount of time associated with each element on the flow diagram. For example, the time spent waiting in queue can be captured by marking the time and date on a product or report as it enters and exits a staging or inventory storage area. Next, the elemental times are aligned from longest to shortest (Pareto analysis), and attention is focused on the longest 20%.

Design and map a new process. There are four parts to this step:

Reduce or eliminate non-value-added time. Readily apparent non-value-added time includes waiting for approvals, waiting for information, waiting in queue, or waiting for tools, material, or equipment.

Reduce or eliminate non-value-added activity. This includes rework, repair, inspection, or transportation.

Switch from sequential to parallel activities. The timing of work activities should be rearranged to maximize what is done in parallel and to minimize what is done sequentially. Parallel work may require more people for short periods of time.

Investigate applications of information technology. Information technology can eliminate the time taken to transfer information from one location to another.

Try out the new process. Run an off-line trial of the revised process to work out the bugs.

Refine by analyzing and problem-solving. When no more non-value-added time or activity can be easily identified, the procedure should be repeated from the beginning: observe and map the process; collect time data; perform a Pareto analysis of the elemental times; and identify the barriers to reducing the longest 20%. A structured approach to problem-solving can then be used in order to develop solutions to overcome the barriers.

Standardize. It's important to hold the gains. This is done by documenting the process and by training everyone involved in implementation of the new procedures. This is where ISO 9000, which requires documentation of work-process changes, meshes well with performance-improvement initiatives.

Continuously improve. In an environment of continuous improvement, there will always be a better way.

A cascading approach

If a cascading approach is taken to the reduction of cycle times, there is very little chance of suboptimal improvements, such as reducing cycle times of one subprocess by pushing activities to another subprocess. A cascading approach simply means beginning with high-level, cross-functional processes, and then systematically involving the people who perform the work in the development of ways to reduce the times of the most lengthy subprocesses.

Benefits in key areas

Cycle time reduction yields results in several key areas:
- greater flexibility and quicker response to customer needs;
- increased capacity,
- enhanced problem-solving,
- higher inventory turns,
- improved quality,
- increased productivity, and
- reduced costs.

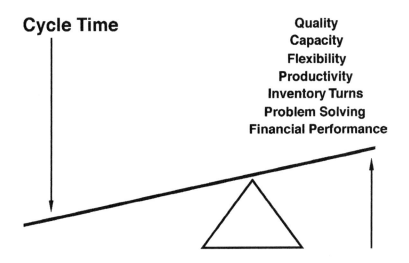

Cycle Time

Quality
Capacity
Flexibility
Productivity
Inventory Turns
Problem Solving
Financial Performance

Not surprisingly, the results are dramatic when companies focus their process-improvement efforts on reducing cycle times. Some better-known examples of companies which have achieved such results are Federal Express, Harley-Davidson, Motorola, General Electric, Wal-Mart, and Toyota.

Reducing cycle times is the means of achieving fast response, which is one of the core values and concepts identified by the Baldridge criteria as the foundation for integrating customer satisfaction and company performance.

Yes, baseball is America's national pastime, and managers use sports analogies when discussing business strategies. But when it comes to how Americans actually function in the workplace, teams and teamwork are foreign to our heritage and our culture. For decades we have recognized and rewarded people as individuals, not as members of a team. Our values and our compensation systems also reinforce individual performance.

Yet effective teamwork is the primary means by which a company can involve its people in its efforts to achieve truly high performance. It's up to leadership to create and nurture an environment that makes it possible for teams to succeed.

It took years for U.S. businesses to learn this lesson. As early as the 1960s, they began to send groups to Japan to study what had enabled the Japanese to rebuild their industries so quickly and so successfully after World War II. Americans saw outward manifestations, such as quality circles and robots, and tried to transplant them into the American workplace. But Americans failed to realize that techniques such as the extensive use of teamwork are intrinsic to Japanese culture and that they developed from basic centuries-old needs.

Supporting structures and techniques

Teams don't happen naturally in our culture. In order for teams to work in American industry, they need a supporting structure. The ultimate goal, of course, is to transform the environment so that teams function naturally without the need of special support. But first, to get teams formed and functioning effectively, the organization needs to build an infrastructure that has the following elements:

Steering Committee. This leadership group creates the environment and sees to it that all the appropriate conditions for success are in place, including direction, priorities, resources, support, and recognition. In effect, the committee is literally steering the organization away from old, deeply ingrained habits toward significantly different behaviors.

Training. This involves group dynamics as well as the tools and techniques of performance improvement. Training is needed for team members and for those who need to support the teams, starting with the steering committee. Team members, leaders, and facilitators need training in group dynamics and in the tools appropriate to their task. When all employees are trained in team skills and group dynamics, they will have a much better understanding of how to interact with teams and how to support them. When team members are trained in facilitation, they will have a much better understanding of what the facilitator is trying to do for them.

The basic foundation of skills for any team is the effective use of divergent and convergent thinking, or the ability to create ideas and to make decisions. The tools that enable a team to do this are brainstorming and consensus, which we discussed in detail earlier in this chapter. Beyond brainstorming and consensus, a team that is chartered to solve a problem needs to have a good working knowledge of a problem-solving model and a process-improvement model, which also were discussed in earlier chapters.

Process improvement models identify the most significant opportunities for improvement (problems) in any work process. In order to avoid suboptimal improvements, an analysis of the entire work process via a process improvement methodology should be done before any problem-solving begins.

At first this analysis may be done by the steering committee, which assigns problems to teams or forms teams to address identified problems. As teams progress to the more advanced stages of empowerment and select their own problems, teams will need training in process improvement.

Skilled facilitation. Facilitators have an extremely important role to play in creating effective teams. This was discussed in an earlier chapter. Suffice it to say here that a facilitator is *not* a member of a team and is *not* involved in content. Rather, a facilitator *is* involved with process, and thus provides the team with tools, techniques, and guidance. Facilitators need training in order to perform their role effectively. They need to know the appropriate tool for the task at hand, they train teams to use tools effectively, and they lead teams in the application of the tools.

Appropriate environment. To be effective, a team cannot work in a vacuum. It needs the cooperation and support of others in the organization. Cooperation and support includes access to information and other salient resources which may not have been provided previously. For example, an hourly employee may be assigned by the team to go to the accountant for data not routinely provided to hourly employees.

Maturation as a team. Each team needs to progress through a maturation process known as forming, storming, norming, and performing. The team must complete each phase before it can progress to the next. If, for example, a team doesn't work through the storming phase, it will remain stalled in the polite first phase of forming and will not develop the real power that stems from the interaction of a mature team.

Time. Teams need time in two respects. First, the maturation process described above takes time. Second, the problem-solving itself takes time. If the organization can wait for the results, teams will usually develop less complex, less expensive, more creative, and more effective solutions to creative problems than will individual technical experts. Most teams meet for an hour a week; part of that hour is needed to bring members up to date and to report on work assignments done outside the meeting time. At one hour per week, it takes a team about three months to perform eight hours of work on a project. More urgent problems will need more time.

Receptivity. The people who will approve the team's ideas need to be open-minded and receptive to their recommendations. This will grow out of an understanding that the solution that will work best will be the one that is created and owned by the people who have to implement it. Conversely, if there are preconceived ideas about what the solution should be, a team should not be asked to solve the problem.

Reward and recognition. People need to feel that their contributions are genuinely appreciated and that they are not being exploited. Management must be prepared to answer the question, "What's in it for me?" This subject is discussed in detail in the chapter on compensation and recognition.

The right problems for groups

It's important to know what types of problems groups should be given—or not given—to solve. First, groups or teams, not individuals, are ideally suited to solving creative problems, *not* analytical ones. An analytical problem is one that has a single solution that is practical and fail-safe. A lot of technical expertise might be required, but given that expertise, the solution is straightforward.

A creative problem, on the other hand, has typically been around for years because it has no single, fail-safe solution; if it had, it would have been solved long ago.

The secret is to put an individual expert, such as an engineer, to work on analytical problems, and to put teams to work on creative problems. To do the opposite is counterproductive. When an expert is given a creative problem, the solution developed is usually more complex and expensive than a team's solution would be. This happens because the solution has to be fail-safe, and it has to be fail-safe because it won't necessarily have the support of the people who have to implement it.

The right people to solve the problems

Fixing a faucet requires the right tool for the job and the ability to use it. It's much the same with teams. Whether the team already exists or it's being formed specifically for the problem at hand, it's important to assess team membership in relation to the type of problem the team will address. There are three criteria to consider:
1. Do the team members have first-hand knowledge of the problem?
2. Do the team members deal directly with the problem?
3. Does the team have control? That is, can one or more members implement the solution without external approval?

The answers to these questions identify the type of problem in relation to the team, and the degree of probability that the team will achieve a successful solution.

Type I problem. The group is high in all three of the above criteria. The team has first-hand knowledge of the problem, members must deal with it directly, and the team can implement its solution without external approval. Chances of success are high; solutions will be developed quickly, and the team will find the process highly gratifying.

Type II. The group is high in one or two of the three criteria, and it is typically low in control. Many problems seem to fall into this category. Chances of success are good if the problem is approached correctly.

Type III. The group is low in all three of the criteria. Failure is likely, and team frustration will be high. In the end, even if the team is successful, it will have solved someone else's problem. Groups should be discouraged from working on Type III problems.

Teams: the most misunderstood element

Effective teams are the heart and soul of any high-performance organization. Yet we have seen that the most misunderstood element of implementation is when and how to use teams, and what it takes to make teams effective. This seems to hold true regardless of the size or type of organization.

Moreover, frustration with ineffective teams is often what causes management to give up on its continuous improvement efforts. The ability to make teams effective will make or break an organization's efforts to improve performance.

We don't know of any high-performing organization that began its improvement initiatives simply by forming teams, nor do we know of any organization that became high-performing without having truly effective teams. Teams must be formed within the context of a long-range plan for improvement which in turn must be an integral part of the overall strategic plan.

Finally, team success is a deceptively complex phenomenon. What works well in one culture won't necessarily work in another. In Japan, for example, the culture supports teams, and they form naturally as problems arise. In our culture, teams usually will not work effectively without careful planning, training, and an understanding of what cultural traits contribute to their success. Even within the U.S. and within a given industry, what works for one company may not work for another. Many things—such as the level of trust, the management style, the appraisal system, the current financial condition, how secure people feel in their jobs, and past experience with teams—all play a part in determining what needs to be done to make teams effective.

The infrastructure we have described throughout this book will create the necessary foundation for effective teams. Beyond that, every organization needs to take into consideration its own unique culture as it makes plans to organize, train, and support teams. This foundation will maximize the effectiveness of the teams, and their effectiveness will determine the success of the organization's efforts to improve performance. Shortcuts won't work.

In discussing continuous improvement, we talk a lot about empowerment. We need to take time to examine the concept behind this word, which often evokes strong responses, both positive and negative.

At one end of the continuum is the traditional style of management, where top management gives the orders and makes the decisions. At the other end of the continuum we find the new style of management. Here we find real employee commitment to the goals of the organization, and employees empowered to make decisions about how they will carry out their work and create greater customer satisfaction. There are seven steps or stages along this continuum.

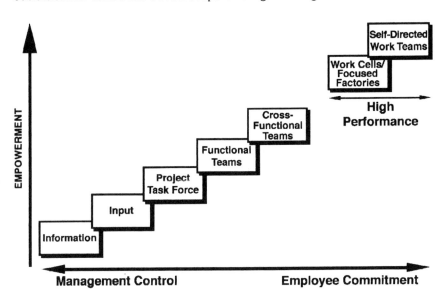

Information. This is the first small but vital step toward increased empowerment. At this stage, top management shares with employees information that has traditionally been held in confidence. This is usually a one-way transaction.

Input. Here top management says, "We have a decision to make. We are the ones who will make the decision, but we want to know what you think before we decide." Top management maintains slightly less control because asking for input carries some obligation to consider the comments offered.

Task force. Management brings together a group of employees to implement a decision that management has made. The task force usually has some latitude in determining how the decision will be implemented. There is slightly less management control, which results in slightly more employee commitment.

Problem-solving team. This stage is the beginning of teams as we usually see them chartered in the early stages of employee involvement. A problem-solving team, sometimes called a functional problem-solving team, consists of members from one functional area or department. It may be given a problem, or it may select a problem within its work area. The team may or may not have a manager as one of its members. In either case, the solutions the team develops usually require approval by a member of management who is not part of the group.

Cross-functional problem-solving team. This team includes people from different departments and different levels in the organization. By virtue of its composition, a cross-functional team works on problems or processes that are broader in scope. Because it often has one or more managers as team members, it is generally more empowered simply by virtue of the authority those members possess. The team is therefore able to have greater impact and more control over implementation of its recommendations. This is as far as most organizations get with empowerment.

The gap. We don't consider any of the types of empowerment described so far to be high-performance work teams. The teams described up to this point usually meet for an hour or two per week, when they look at problems after the fact. It is a leap—not a step—to the next levels on the continuum. Work cells and self-directed work teams are cross-functional *work* groups, whose members work together on a real-time basis: day to day, hour to hour, minute to minute. They are structured both physically and organizationally to focus on a customer or a group of customers, on a product or a group of products, or on a cross-functional work process. These groups have a high degree of impact on customer satisfaction and on operational performance.

Work cell (focused factory). This is a cross-functional group of people who work together to perform a function or to produce a product or service. They are focused on consistently meeting or exceeding their customers' expectations. All members learn all jobs in the cell and often rotate among all jobs. Members work on small lots, can see what others are doing, and react quickly to nonconformances. A work cell is organized like a small factory within a larger factory, with dedicated resources and support staff. Members work together toward a common end and can see the result of their work. This arrangement fosters pride in the finished product. All members are building quality into the product as they work. The need for an inspection function is eliminated because all members inspect 100% of the product as they produce it, and they receive immediate feedback as they hand it off to the next worker. In many cases the product goes directly from the work cell to an external customer.

In contrast, one company, after three years of continuous improvement efforts, said one of its greatest successes was organized employee tours of various parts of the plant. A welder who had worked at the company for 30 years said he saw his internal customer, the assembly department, for the first time on such a tour. This company was just beginning to scratch the surface of customer focus. If employees don't know how their work affects their internal customer, they can't possibly know if it satisfies the external customer. A work cell effectively overcomes this problem.

Self-directed work team. The major difference between a work cell and a self-directed work team is the level of empowerment. Members of a self-directed work team, in addition to designing, performing, and improving their own work, often make on-the-spot decisions to satisfy customers. They operate with little or no supervision. Each team member understands every other team member's role. Members develop teamwork skills and use various tools of process improvement and problem-solving. Because the team has ownership in the way the work is done, the team is committed to high-performance results. The team manages itself. Managers no longer direct and control; they coach and facilitate the team.

The star system

The star system (originated by the Hannaford brothers) can serve as a model for delegating authority and responsibility to self-directed work teams. Leadership identifies the areas of authority and accountability (or the star points) and spells out the boundaries of authority in detail. An organization may have a star with any number of points; Saturn, for example, had 35 at last count.

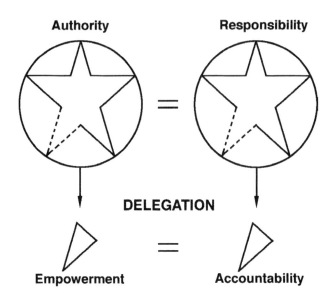

Typically, each star point has a leader. He or she serves as the contact for others in the organization and also as the coordinator of team activities relative to this area of responsibility.

A common misperception, and a frequent pitfall in implementation, is the belief that empowerment is an all-or-nothing proposition. It's important to note that regardless of how many points exist and how many of them are delegated, a team receives only the amount of authority and responsibility that leadership has specifically defined. The balance of authority, represented by the space between the star points, remains the responsibility of management.

Changing role of management

The role of management, specifically of first-line and middle managers, requires careful consideration and needs to be clearly defined before implementing self-directed work teams. This is an issue of job security.

If the reason for implementing self-directed work teams is to eliminate a layer of management, the real benefits of such teams may never be realized. We have found situations where teams are ineffective even though all support systems are in place with one vital exception: managers don't see a role for themselves in the new organization, and they are therefore threatened by it.

Supervisors get justifiably concerned when they see their former responsibilities being performed by other people. If the new supervisory role is not clearly defined, then the more successful self-direction becomes, the more tenuous the supervisors' position seems in the new organization. If they aren't coordinating and controlling daily work, supervisors see little left for them to do.

Supervisors need to understand the new system and their part in it. A former supervisor may become a team leader or the team trainer. A former shift or division manager may become a coordinator, with overall responsibility for coaching and facilitating an area with two or more teams.

The configuration and terminology vary from one organization to another, but the role of the first-line supervisor usually becomes one of trainer, facilitator, coach, and coordinator. This is an entirely new role, and new types of behavior are required. This transition doesn't happen quickly or easily, and leadership needs to provide the tools and the support to enable managers to make the transition physically and mentally.

Reap the benefits

Companies that have maximum levels of empowerment and that successfully implement self-directed work teams are organized to truly utilize the full potential and creativity of their people. Such companies have more satisfied customers and more satisfied employees. There is a direct link between the two. These companies are structured for continuous improvement and equipped to meet the competitive challenges of the future.

It takes time, patience, and perseverance, but the end result is well worth the investment: an organization committed and empowered to meet the competitive challenges of the future.

ABOUT THE PROFILES

In selecting companies for our *Profiles*, we looked for as diverse a cross-section as possible.

First, these companies range widely in size and sales. L-S Electro-Galvanizing Company has the fewest people, 93. Picker International and Republic Engineered Steels have 4,400 and 4,500, respectively; and University Hospitals of Cleveland has more than 7,000.

Zircoa has one location. Pioneer-Standard Electronics has 53 U.S. branches and a Canadian subsidiary; and Picker has 11 major locations worldwide.

In companies where sales figures apply, annual sales range from $18 million for Zircoa to $1.0 billion for Picker and $1.3 billion for Pioneer-Standard.

While most of these companies are in manufacturing, where high-performance efforts have the longest history, we also include distribution (Pioneer-Standard) and health care (University Hospitals of Cleveland).

More important, all nine companies serve as outstanding examples of successful implementation of many of the various elements of high-performance work systems. In this regard, the *Profiles* provide the kind of information that would be gathered on a benchmarking visit.

Ford Engine Plant 2 came back from a lights-out situation, reinvented itself, and has become a leading producer of high-quality engines.

L-S Electro-Galvanizing Company is a joint venture of LTV Steel and Sumitomo Metal Industries. Independent of its American and Japanese parents, L-SE created a modern operating agreement with the United Steel Workers of America.

Picker International has a unique quality-improvement system which benchmarks three models, and an outstanding annual reward and recognition event, called a Qualithon.

Pioneer-Standard Electronics has developed and executed a comprehensive, fully integrated plan for performance improvement and exceptional growth.

Republic Engineered Steels was born as an Employee Stock Ownership Plan and has an extensive program of business education, also known as Open Book Management.

Rexroth Mobile Hydraulics illustrates the achievement of ISO certification in a company with a highly complex and customized manufacturing process.

University Hospitals of Cleveland applied one of the basic tools of performance improvement, namely process mapping and standardization, in the development of care paths.

Van Dorn Demag implemented a total quality improvement program and made a successful turnaround to become competitive internationally.

Zircoa has answered the question, "What's in it for me?" with an outstanding gain sharing program. The company also has a very extensive program of employee training and education.

Read and reflected upon alongside the *Prescriptions*, these *Profiles* offer inspiration and insight into the practicalities involved in creating high-performance work systems.

FORD CLEVELAND ENGINE PLANT 2

Location: Brook Park, Ohio.

Site Manager: Gifford M. Brown.

People: 1,016.

History: Opened in 1955. Engine Plant 2 produced over a million engines in 1959, but by the mid-1980s operations had been reduced to the point that the lights had gone out. In 1989, however, the plant earned Ford's Q1 award and went on to be selected to build the high-tech engines for Ford's first world cars.

The plant occupies 1.2 million square feet of manufacturing space; it is located on a 365-acre site, with Cleveland Engine Plant 1 and Cleveland Casting Plant.

Management of Engine Plant 2, together with its union, the United Auto Workers Local #1250, developed a comprehensive production strategy. Called the Cleveland Production System, it is very similar to the system that has since been adopted by Ford.

The plant won the Workplace Star Award in 1994 from the U.S. Department of Labor and the Shingo Prize in 1996 for Excellence in Manufacturing. The 2.5-liter engine was named one of the top ten engines in 1995 by *Ward's Auto World*.

Business: This plant produces the 2.5-liter and 3.0-liter V-6 Duratec engine, a small and lightweight engine that is virtually carefree, designed to go 100,000 miles between tuneups. The 2.5-liter engine is used in the Mercury Mystique, Ford Contour, and European Ford Mondeo; the 3.0-liter engine is used in the Ford Taurus and Mercury Sable.

Output capacity (annual): 415,000 units.

Commentary

Back in the 1960s, about one car in 100 was made overseas. Within 20 years, more than 30 cars in 100 were designed and built overseas. Today both Europe and Japan make more cars than we do. U.S. automakers lost a lot of ground in a short time. Blame was placed on short-sighted management, contentious unions, and an unresponsive government.

But the time for placing blame is long over. Companies that haven't already begun responding to the new global economics may find it's too late to start. For now U.S. companies like Ford and U.S. plants like Cleveland Engine Plant 2 are catching and passing even the best of the Japanese and European plants.

It's true of course that Ford has considerable resources to apply to this type of venture. But as we have seen time and again in auto and other industries, capital alone will not provide strategic competitiveness. Money and advanced technology cannot provide the vision that captures people's imaginations and builds trust between management and workforce.

Ford managers and members of UAW Local #1250 at Engine Plant 2 have *together* created a single mission. With this one mission as its foundation, Engine Plant 2 presents a single front to a stormy global economic climate. This foundation of mutual cooperation and trust has led directly to the plant's renewal.

Organizations can no longer afford the luxury of getting only a little better. All manufacturers, particularly in the auto industry, must get much better along many dimensions very quickly. And they are finding that they simply cannot do it with traditional systems and methods.

You can get new tires and tune the engine, but to win the Indy 500, you must rebuild the car from the ground up. In the 1960s, U.S. car manufacturers had the track all to themselves; now they are competing in a global Indy 500. Ford and Engine Plant 2 clearly intend to be in the winner's circle. They are building the high-performance engine for today and tomorrow.

Engine Plant 2 found a new way of doing business. It's based on simple things: cooperation, listening, sharing ideas and information, and the straightforward idea that the people making the engines are in the best position to figure out the best way to do it.

The Cleveland Production System is a comprehensive and rigorous approach. It works because it's based on a spirit of cooperation and trust, and because it starts and ends with the needs of customers and employees. It truly empowers employees on the line. Employees have developed a system surprisingly simple and wonderfully comprehensive. They have successfully met one of the toughest challenges for any organization—to remake itself. And they have done it in a short amount of time.

—WINOC

At its peak of production in 1959, Cleveland Engine Plant 2 employed 3,000 workers who produced over a million engines. But hard times came, and by the mid-1980s the plant, with a workforce of at most 400, was reduced to a few machining operations and to use as a warehouse. The lights had gone out.

Ford offered the plant a chance to acquire an engine program if UAW Local #1250 would implement a Modern Operating Agreement. The union, which had a national reputation for toughness, voted down the agreement, confident the plant would get the engine anyway.

When the engine went elsewhere, management and labor began talking in earnest about working together. For the first time, they looked at the plant and its future, saw the same scenario, and agreed on what needed to be done. They decided to pursue Ford's Q1 award, which requires much training in Statistical Quality Control and other topics, as well as meeting and maintaining rigorous quality standards. The plant won the award in 1989.

A new era is born

In 1988 a new 6-cylinder engine program became available. Ford intended to build a world car, with a powerful but small and light engine, and to build it on U.S. soil. When Engine Plant 2 requested the program, Ford repeated its previous condition: implement a Modern Operating Agreement, which includes a number of radically different concepts in labor-management relations, including a relaxation in work rules that gives management more flexibility in assigning workers.

In 1989 UAW Local #1250 and site management formulated a modern operating conceptual agreement. This two-page document committed plant management and the union to work together in new ways. Based on it, Ford awarded the program to Engine Plant 2.

UAW Local #1250 and Ford site leadership began working jointly toward the goal of building the system by which they would manufacture the new engine. The Operating Committee, composed of union and management, developed a Mission Statement for this new team approach to manufacturing. It focuses employees on a common goal of building a world-class engine and on removing labor-management barriers.

The Operating Committee translated the Mission Statement into concrete objectives and action. "What We Stand For," a two-page document, outlined what the plant intended to accomplish, how accomplishments would be measured, and what methods and tools would be used to attain the goals.

Cleveland Production System

To begin developing what would become the Cleveland Production System, the Operating Committee benchmarked a number of manufacturing sites: Toyota in Georgetown, KY, and in Japan; Mazda in Flat Rock, MI; NUUMI in Fremont, CA; and Ford plants across the U.S. It became clear that most of the other companies' sites had something Ford didn't: a cohesive and comprehensive system for making a product. Also, the very best systems were consistently based on three themes, or pillars: effective integration of workers and technology through empowerment; a just-in-time approach; and a commitment to adding value and eliminating all waste. These three pillars are reflected in the Cleveland Production System.

New hires came mainly from Engine Plant 1 and layoff rolls. All new hires were told what was expected of them per the mission statement and received more than 100 hours of training upon hire.

Many of the first rehires in 1991 were assigned to Simultaneous Engineering Teams made up of line managers, engineers, and workers represented by the United Auto Workers Local #1250. The Simulteams were to design, purchase, install, and make operational the new systems and equipment. These teams made a tremendous contribution to the success of Engine Plant 2.

Simulteams design systems

Each team identified a series of potential vendors for the systems to be purchased. At this point the vendors did not have a purchase agreement; they worked with the teams and gave them ideas for equipment design. The teams spent weeks away from home working with these vendors. At the same time, the teams benchmarked other operations to develop equipment standards. The experience can be described in the words of Neil Reddy, who was a member of one of the Simulteams.

"We would work for 9 or 10 hours at the vendor, go eat together and still keep working on improvements. Then we would sit around together after supper, still discussing what we were trying to accomplish. We worked hard together. We really were a team. We became like a military squad that supports and watches out for one another. We had lots of arguments and disagreements. That's what it was all about, everybody adding in his thoughts and ideas, not holding back. That's how we got the system we have today.

"I remember in particular one sharp disagreement over the configuration of a particular component we were designing. I was on one side, but finally I said, 'Hey, let's go look at this thing some more. Let's get back with the vendors and get some more information.' We did, and we were able to come to agreement. The important point was that we got to consensus by talking, listening, and digging up good information. We came to trust each other that decisions weren't going to be made on any basis other than what we could show was the best design and best process."

Once the equipment was designed and the orders placed, team members stayed on-site with the vendors as the equipment was built, working with it and testing it. As machinery entered the finishing and shipping stage, some team members returned to the plant to begin installation.

When the Simulteams had the lines installed and running, team members began producing engines on a trial basis. One engine at a time was built and fully inspected, then 10 engines, then 30, then more. Also, the teams made the transition from the intensive and creative phase of building the line to the day-by-day mindset of running the line.

The goal of Engine Plant 2 is to manufacture engines that are best-in-class in quality and cost through the effective and efficient use of resources. The Cleveland Production System is based on the concept that these goals will be achieved through the maintenance of the highest-quality relationships.

The change at Cleveland is an important step in Ford's move away from mass production, regimented work, centralized authority, push delivery systems, and inventory buffers. The transition to modern production will lead to:

- delivering to customers what they want,
- producing effectively and efficiently at lower production volumes,
- incorporating employees and suppliers fully as part of the system, and
- continuously improving performance, quality, cost, and productivity.

Work teams

Employees are assigned to work teams. The teams are expected to keep the lines stocked and running, to carry out simple maintenance, and to solve problems. Any team member may stop the line because of a quality problem, and they do so. Every team member rotates through all of the jobs in the team each day. Rotation is a key component of the teams' success: it spells the end of entire days spent on a single job which is tiresome. It has also resulted in the willingness of all team members to ergonomically improve each of the jobs.

Ergonomics are vastly important in the auto industry, which has some of the highest rates of muscular and skeletal injuries. Most of the ergonomic solutions here were developed by the teams, not by outside experts. The lines are designed to be run by virtually anyone, regardless of size.

Work teams have an average of 5 to 10 members. Each team selects one of its members to serve as the coordinator. To be eligible, a worker must have demonstrated the ability to perform all team jobs and must have exemplary people skills. A coordinator serves for six months. The job is tough.

The coordinator is important to the success of the team. He or she must know the production schedule, assign jobs, make sure the line has stock, facilitate weekly work team meetings, and serve as communication channel and liaison with the rest of the organization. The work teams are empowered to set up their own operating rules, to implement solutions, and to make improvements to the work design.

Coordinators report to Manufacturing Advisors, who come from engineering, production supervision, and other backgrounds. About the job, one advisor comments, "We're coach, facilitator, and teacher to the teams and coordinators. The idea is for the teams to do all of these things well enough so that they don't need us any longer. After all, they know their jobs better than we ever did. We still spend a lot of time on the floor, but we are gathering information that helps us plan for the longer term, focusing on things like continual improvement, cost reduction, and safety."

Manufacturing Advisors report to a Team Manager. For example, Neil Reddy, a former Simulteam member, is now Team Manager in Cylinder Block Machining, where he is assisted by two Manufacturing Advisors, a Coordinator, and a work team of eight.

Visual factory and instant access

Engine Plant 2 is extraordinarily clean. The floor, walls, and all machine surfaces fairly gleam. It's also quiet. A goal is to run at below 80 decibels, not much louder than a typical office. And everyone looks relaxed. Nobody shouts or scurries about. It can be difficult to believe this plant makes engines of as high a quality and as efficiently as any in the nation.

The plant puts an emphasis on the concept of visual factory, the use of visual cues to communicate and direct operations. For example, the andon board, a large electric display hanging from the ceiling, signals when a station is up and running (a green circle) or down (a red X). A quick glance at the board tells anyone the operating status of the entire line.

A computer console next to each line gives everyone immediate access to a wealth of diagnostic information about what's going on within the line. At each machine, a computer terminal provides not only a quick diagnosis of problems but also gives information about tool wear and remaining tool life, so tooling changes can be made quickly and at the most opportune time, preventing machine downtime.

Through computers, all operators have constant access to a wide variety of up-to-the-minute performance data: a Pareto analysis of downtime by cause, a table of Mean Time Between Events (problems), and so on. People are expected to use the data for continual improvement.

Near almost every manual work station is an assortment of laminated diagrams, instruction sheets, and other job aids with easy-to-find, easy-to-read instructions and information. Developed by the team, these job aids contain just about anything a technician needs to know about a particular work station.

The Dimensional Control Planning (DCP) system is intended to control quality problems at the source and as they happen. This is the simplest, most effective, and least expensive way. DCP is a straightforward tactic: list the steps of a process, anticipate potential problems in each step, and develop responses to those potential problems. Again, team members develop DCP standards and update them as line configurations change.

Closely related to the DCP system is the Quality Process System (QPS), which has been sustained as a primary channel for worker input into continual improvement of line efficiency. Central to the system is stopwatch measurement and detailed documentation of each task on the line. As these methods are historically associated with work speedups and job eliminations, employee emotions ran high in the early days of QPS. But it has proven itself to be useful and nonthreatening.

Preventing problems

Much attention has been given to preventing problems before they occur. There's a great variety of Poka-yoke ideas, or mistake-proofing. For example, a metal plate hanging over the line is cut in the shape of the proper piece that will pass beneath it; if the piece is misaligned, it hits the plate and triggers a relay that in turn stops the line.

Empowering workers to take control of the design and flow of the work is not as easy as simply telling workers they are empowered; workers must get real-time information—and lots of it—about what's going on, and they must have done some thinking ahead of time about how to respond to those problems. Manufacturing Advisors and Team Managers welcome this kind of empowerment, saying, "We love it. Everything is kept right here at the floor level." A Team Coordinator says, "If I could point to the one thing that has made the most difference, it's the sincere desire on the company's part to hear from us."

The problem-solving approach follows up on the Modern Operating Agreement. This Agreement replaced the thick manual spelling out rules for every imaginable situation. In the words of Team Manager Ron Beckler, "Now we focus on what's the right thing, the moral thing to do in each situation, and the employees are a part of this discussion. We simply start the conversation about any problem by asking what's the best way to approach it."

The plant runs lean on inventory. This puts a lot of stress on internal communication systems. The team coordinator is central to communication: he or she is in constant contact with lift drivers, team members, and other coordinators.

Coordinators communicate with other coordinators and team members by radio. Over time, coordinators have learned that keeping an ear on all radio conversation is the best way to keep up with what's going on at all points on the line.

People make the difference

Ford has spent more than a billion dollars to produce this engine, and it may look as if the manufacture of these engines is controlled basically by computers and robots. Yet it's quite apparent that everything would come to a halt, worth only the price of scrap, if not for the teams. The way they plan, communicate, and resolve problems seems to be the real secret to the success of the Cleveland Production System.

"Companies think they need the best technology, that they need to be faster and quicker, that they need to have more dollars or spend the least dollars," says Gifford Brown, Site Manager. "But technology and facilities come and go. What really makes the difference is utilization and optimization of the individuals within the organization. They must be motivated, aligned, and focused on goals in order to be well utilized. Most organizations are 15-20% utilized at best."

A Manufacturing Advisor, Kevin Bigley, says: "Five years ago, I spent my time running around fighting fires. Now, when the line is down, team members identify the problem and do what they can to fix it themselves. We know that occasionally people make mistakes in their solutions and decisions, but we take the position that we're all learning as we go with this system. In the old days, workers sat and waited for a supervisor to arrive and provide a correction when the line went down. The supervisor reinforced that behavior by doing just what the workers expected: he moved the worker out of the way and tackled the problem himself, maybe with an engineer, but not with the employee. Now work-team members do what they need to do to keep the line going."

"In the new type of management," says Brown, "management is still responsible but has to share authority. "The manager's role is expanded: the manager has to educate, to have good rationale, and to answer questions that never had to be answered before. That makes it more difficult. It works, but *only* by focusing on goals; otherwise, things unravel. Goals are the glue holding together two groups from different sides of the table. Our management team grew in this transition. Many of them grew a *lot*."

Results tell the story

Cleveland Engine Plant 2 has been building the 2.5-liter engine for two years and the 3.0-liter engine for just a year. Is it fair to compare the performance of these engines with others that have been in production for more than a decade? Doesn't it take a few years to work the bugs out of any system? Engine Plant 2 invites just that sort of comparison.

"We've been putting together data that show our launch was perhaps one of the most successful in the industry," says Chris Bolen, Quality Planning Manager. "Certainly, it was the best launch in Ford. We can show that the philosophy put into practice here works. A few results back up my statement that our launch will be seen as the benchmark.

"One important measure is body and assembly engine pulls per thousand engines. Our immediate customer is the assembly plant. We count how many times an engine installed by the assembly plant has to be removed because of a quality problem. Engine pulls are obviously an additional cost in building the car. Moreover, they are symptomatic of problems with the engine itself.

"Right now our plant's engine pulls per thousand for both the 3.0-liter and the 2.5-liter are equal to similar Ford engines that have been manufactured at other plants for six years in one case and eleven years in another. This is seen as nearly incredible performance. Today's methodology for identifying bad engines is much more sophisticated and rigorous than it was when those engines were launched, so in a way we had a higher hurdle to get over. And the reports we get from the Body and Assembly plants have been very positive."

The plant also counts engine exchanges. If a car buyer has a problem that can only be fixed by opening the engine, the dealer simply puts in a new engine and sends the original one back to the plant. This procedure led to the quick identification and correction of two significant problems with the 2.5-liter engine soon after launch. Engine exchanges per thousand dropped about 90% from last year to this year.

Another important yardstick is the number of engines in purchased automobiles that must be repaired in the first three months of service. The performance of the 3.0-liter engine immediately after launch was equal to that of another Ford engine that has been in production for eleven years.

The plant's joint approach to designing and installing the new systems also resulted in substantial financial benefits. Ford calculated an investment savings of $400 million in the engine launch.

Engine Plant 2's exemplary performance has also been noticed by many outside Ford. U.S. Labor Secretary Robert Reich presented Cleveland Engine Plant 2 with the Workplace Star Award in 1994. A new customer satisfaction survey by J.D. Power and Associates ranked the 2.5-liter engine second-best in the U.S., beating both Honda and Toyota. And in 1996 the plant won the coveted Shingo Prize for Excellence in Manufacturing.

The best recognition of all comes from Ford itself. Ford has chosen Cleveland Engine Plant 2 to make an additional version of the Duratec engine to go into new designs of Jaguars and a new luxury vehicle for Ford. Nearly $200 million will be invested in the plant for this purpose.

The benefits of the Cleveland Production System are clear and tangible. The plant achieved the best engine launch in Ford's history, perhaps in automotive history, and quality indicators have reached remarkable levels for an engine that has been in production for a relatively short period of time.

A matter of goals and trust

"The issue of trust," says Brown, "has never been evaluated or emphasized enough. If you do all these things right, the natural outcome is that everybody has trust. When you don't do things right or explain things, you erode the foundation of trust. Then distrust and adversarial feelings can be so strong that people work against you.

"Everything we have accomplished here could be destroyed in weeks or minutes. All it would take, for example, is for a manager to make a decision that would generate mistrust. If that happens, I have to reverse the decision, and the manager has to be strong enough to understand and to tell his people he made a bad decision. The result is another notch of trust.

"It all goes back to trust, integrity, communication, and understanding that individuals want to be successful. It requires philosophy, organization, and a support structure. You can't get any of that with capital spending, early retirement, and so on. It's free. It's simple. It's the basic foundation of why things work."

L-S Electro-Galvanizing Company

Location: Cleveland, Ohio.

Executive Vice President: Donald R. Vernon.

People: 93, all salaried.

History: Founded in 1985 as a joint venture of LTV Steel, Cleveland, and Sumitomo Metal Industries (SMI), Japan; independent of both parent companies.

                 Launched by unique labor agreement with United Steel Workers of America Local #9126 that left details of planning and operation to be decided by the participative process involving all employees. Production began in April, 1986; first million tons produced by August, 1989.

                 Continual improvements occur in all areas measured; 1989-1994 figures include a 22% increase in productivity, 33% decrease in production costs, and 99% decrease in customer claims.

Business: Apply zinc coating to steel (electro-galvanizing process) for exposed automotive applications. The plating line, 890 feet long, can accommodate about a mile of steel strip. Coils weighing up to 60,000 pounds are processed and coated to custom specifications.

Production: 400,000 tons throughput.

Commentary

Many individuals and companies wish for the chance to make a totally fresh start. That opportunity became a reality for the people who created L-S Electro-Galvanizing Company (L-SE) from the ground up. This greenfield site rose in the center of a brownfield—legally and physically separated, totally fenced off from the parent, LTV Steel. Few companies have the luxury of such an opportunity, but all can learn some lessons and apply them. L-SE's experience challenges a number of assumptions and beliefs.

L-SE is independent of both parent companies. It was created in a labor agreement unique to the steel industry. This agreement provided for a highly flexible workforce, a skill-based pay system, financial gain sharing, and job security. There would be no job descriptions, no grievance procedures, and no time clocks.

Hiring and training of all employees, management and union, was also unique. The entire union workforce started on the same date. Employees spent the first months in extensive and significant training in all skills related to the manufacturing process and to all key aspects of problem-solving, high performance, and participative management. The entire team also designed the steady-state company, that is, every aspect of ongoing systems, processes, and procedures after startup was completed and operations were stabilized and up to speed.

Responsibilities traditionally reserved for management—employment, training, scheduling, and work assignments—are carried out by representatives of the entire workforce.

L-SE has been successful in terms of quality, throughput, and workforce skills. L-SE was awarded the 1992 Rochester Institute of Technology (RIT)/USA *Today* Quality Cup. Even more important, in 1991 the partners opened a second plant, L-S II, in Columbus, Ohio, to meet demands for specialty-type coated steel.

—WINOC

In the mid-1980s LTV approached Sumitomo Metal Industries (SMI) with the intent of purchasing the technology for electro-galvanizing steel to produce high-quality rust-resistant steel. Instead, the two companies entered a joint venture: L-SE.

The first question raised by many was how this new venture could maximize its chances for success, given the fact that all U.S. competitors were likely to perfect the electro-galvanizing process in the near future. The answer was that L-SE must score high in the other two areas of customer satisfaction: quality and service.

Despite the fact that it stands in the middle of LTV land, L-SE is totally independent of both parent companies. Making it separate was the vision of LTV's Cole Tremain and USWA's Ed Ball, says Don

Vernon, L-SE's Executive Vice President. "They figured that whatever LTV and the United Steel Workers of America (USWA) had been doing for 50 years was not working. So a separate company and a separate labor contract were created." It was a difficult decision, made with conviction but without the 20/20 vision of hindsight. Many outside individuals at LTV, on both the management and union sides, viewed the venture with skepticism, to say the least.

The contract

Discussions were begun with the USWA. The central goal was the creation of a high-performance organization of employees working in an environment with high levels of trust and respect. Both parties saw an opportunity to achieve real dignity in the workplace.

The resulting Labor Agreement was unique to the industry. Unlike the Basic Steel Labor Agreement, which runs to about 200 pages, the L-SE agreement is only 18 pages, plus 17 pages of appendices. It provides for:

- a salaried workforce, with pay scales based on knowledge and skills acquired;
- a gain sharing system instead of incentive programs;
- job security instead of layoff and recall;
- severance allowance, traditionally reserved for nonunion employees; and
- dispute resolution with an emphasis on problem-solving rather than on the traditional grievance procedure.

Carefully hired workforce

Management was hired first, with emphasis on predicting candidates' success in a participative environment. Those hired were trained in the technical processes of electro-galvanizing and the human skills of participative management.

Management in turn hired the original plant workforce. There were more than 1,400 candidates, mostly laid-off Cleveland LTV steel workers; 45 employees were hired. The hiring process, which was quite extensive, included aptitude testing, previous history screening for team-player types, orientation sessions explaining the new company's intentions, and job-related testing.

"This requires a special type of person," says Cal Tinsley, Plant Manager, "one capable of working in a team environment. It's not for anyone who wants to work in his own corner, do his own job, and go home." Psychological testing and interviewing for indicators went far beyond traditional lines.

Extensive training and planning took place in the first months. Training included problem-solving skills, behavioral science theory, technology, specific manufacturing line training at the sister plant in Japan, basic mechanical and electrical subjects, and operation of equipment.

"The contract left a lot to be determined by all of us," says Vernon. "What did we want this venture to be? Having had a bad taste from the 60s and 70s and 80s, everyone was very excited, labor and management alike. It was very creative."

Early discussions resulted in a statement of eight Individual Needs Goals deemed essential to the long-term success of the venture. Since reaffirmed, the goals can be summed up as follows:

- a fair and responsive atmosphere,
- long-term employment and sufficient income,
- the highest level of health and safety,
- top-quality product and customer satisfaction,
- peak efficiency and reliability of equipment,
- equitable opportunity for individual professional growth,
- attention to detail, consistently applied policies, and clear communication, and
- recognition, reward, and constructive criticism to instill pride, respect, and accomplishment.

The group began by trying to eliminate as many barriers as possible, physical and psychological. The goal is difficult to achieve. Everyone, management or union, comes with his own baggage of background, experience, and perspective. It's difficult to do things in one agreed-upon way—and to like it—even when all want to live in a utopia of trust and respect.

"Most of the steel workers hired had been laid off for one to three years. We were eager and willing to try something different and to work very hard to make that happen," says Tom Zidek, President of Local #9126. When hired by L-SE in 1986, after being laid off for three years, he was Vice President of Local #9126. "We jumped in with both feet. We didn't recognize the magnitude of what we were taking on."

Working in small groups and assisted by an outside consultant, the entire team proceeded to design the steady-state company: this included work stations, staffing requirements, administrative systems, and task analysis.

The team dictated its own needs. The line operates nonstop with five crews, all multi-skilled teams capable of handling all functions, including maintenance. "Our strongest competitor," says Vernon, "has a workforce twice as large as ours; our weakest competitor's workforce is three times the size of ours."

After reaching consensus on the design, the team prepared a startup plan. The team approach was typified by the decision to have everyone identify a startup position based not on personal preference but on what was most helpful for the total startup.

Aggressive training program

Despite differences in individual skill levels at time of startup, the skills of all union workers clustered at or near the basic level in 1986. A new hire quickly learns valuable skills, and in 1-3 years that employee can perform every job on the line, as well as maintenance skills. On achieving the first level, the employee masters added skills in different areas of the plant. Pay increases accompany each block of skills, which are fully spelled out.

Fellow employees do the training and testing for these levels, and grant the approval. When the skills blocks are completed, the employee qualifies as Process Technician. Another block of skills and pay increases lead to achievement of intermediate and advanced levels in electronics and instrumentation or in chemical plant and mechanics.

Thanks to an aggressive training program and low turnover—35 of the original 45 union hires are with L-SE today, and the newest hire has been on board 3 years—all workers are now at or near the top, with advanced skills; pay there is double the base pay. Even at the top of the ladder, training goes on: refresher skills, keeping up with changes, and advancing skills in more areas.

L-SE uses slow periods as an opportunity to train employees. There has never been a layoff; slow periods are also a good time to paint walls, catch up on other work, or hold renewal meetings to review strategy and refuel commitment.

Base rate salary accounts for 70% of pay; gain sharing, based mainly on quality and throughput, accounts for 25%; and profit sharing, often elusive in this industry, accounts for 5%.

Quality control

L-SE emphasizes controlling the process rather than inspecting out bad products. The line is monitored for key input and output attributes. Part of every full crew meeting deals with quality issues. Changes have been made to enhance the product and to reduce customer claims for unsatisfactory product. The Integrated Process Control Committee worked on the problem of dents, which represented a significant portion of claims, which cost over $3 per ton in 1988.

The committee campaigned to inspect and reduce problems. It took several years, but by 1992 claims were reduced to 33 cents per ton, L-SE's benchmark against SMI, and they now stand at 10-20 cents per ton. After solving the problem of dents, the committee turned its attention to eliminating scratches, defects so minor that they did not result in customer claims.

"And I didn't have a thing to do with it except to maintain the environment for success," says Vernon.

Committees and functions

L-SE committees own many functions and responsibilities traditionally reserved for management. They were formed in the early months of production, when many unexpected issues had to be addressed jointly. Members volunteer and come from both union and management; once on a committee, they are trained in the skills that committee requires.

The Hiring Committee was formed when L-SE decided to increase output in response to a competitor's production outage. After training in areas such as interviewing techniques and EEO, this committee reviewed candidates, conducted interviews, decided on the best candidates, and offered them a job.

The Pay and Progression Committee developed a pay-for-skill format, building a virtual roadmap for employees, and the Labor Agreement was modified to be compatible with the committee's plan. Because this committee's decisions deal with a cost of doing business, they are not autonomous or final; they are recommendations to top management.

The Training Committee, an outgrowth of the Pay and Progression Committee, determines training needs and implements training. It has turned out to have exclusively union members and has a representative from each crew.

The Gain Sharing Committee, required by the Labor Agreement, defined gain and how to share it, chose and weighted the determinants, calculated formulas and goals, and decided how to deal with unforeseen external factors. Goals are re-evaluated monthly. Actions need approval of top management.

The Safety Committee has a representative from every crew. It has evolved to achieve some autonomy; monthly it can authorize 32 work hours and up to $1,000 for supplies to correct safety matters.

The Integrated Process Control Committee has integrated statistical process control into the plant process, part of the total effort to identify key input and output variables and to install standards.

The ISO 9000 and QS 9000 Committee grew out of the Integrated Process Control Committee.

The Scheduling Committee has one person from each crew. Its first goal, a schedule that pleased everyone, was unattainable, so members worked to minimize misery. The result: a balance of shift rotation, weekends off, and individual flexibility for all.

The Vacation Scheduling Committee, with one person from each crew, developed a plan that rotates prime time to all team members, a lottery to settle issues of potential conflict, and rules for single days off and for pay instead of time off.

The Packaging and Shipping Committee was formed recently to solve specific problems. It has produced significant efficiencies.

The Customer Concerns Committee, also recently created, visits customers to get their input and to meet with their workers and management, and reports back to everyone at L-SE.

A Social Committee and a Fitness Committee also exist.

Equity and consensus

By structure and through attentive effort, L-SE's system is equitable to everyone, with the same opportunities for scheduling work and vacations, the same opportunities for training and advancement, and the same number of people on every shift.

"We have avoided favoritism, a long-standing concern of unions," says Vernon, "and we don't get, 'That's his job, not mine.' That has really minimized workplace problems and grievances. I used to spend 30% of my time on grievances and other nonproductive issues. We have had only five grievances since 1985, and not one has been to arbitration. Fundamentally, we don't believe in going to an outsider who knows nothing about us, and we don't want to have winners and losers.

"In other companies, a worker advances by joining the grievance committee or becoming a union officer; in our company a worker advances to head a committee. If someone is unhappy with something, we say, 'Change it.' If someone has a better idea, we say, 'Sell it to the group.' People don't argue issues with management but with their peers.

"It's management's responsibility to create an environment conducive to high morale and to support workers and committees by giving them what they need. Our approach is one of daily cooperation rather than daily confrontation, of identifying a problem and asking how we can solve it. We try to keep our identity, to keep close, and to keep a sense of being different.

"There have been frustrations," says Zidek, "like things not happening fast enough, or not always being able to balance the people side and the business side. When you cannot deliver for the people side, it causes anger and frustration, much like in a family when it rains and you can't take your children to the zoo the way you promised."

Joint venture: a difference

Although the entire original team trained and observed in Japan and benchmarked against the Japanese plant, the Ohio venture has its unique plan and operation. Cleveland's flexible work system is so efficient, requiring fewer people, that SMI plans to adopt it in Japan.

The 21 members of L-SE management include two SMI people here on 5-year stints. They take part in all meetings and know members of the workforce. All decisions are made on the basis of what is good for L-SE, separate and distinct from the parent companies.

Still a way to go

In 1993, Tinsley and Zidek took part in Future of the American Workplace Conference, sponsored by President Clinton and the U.S. Department of Labor. L-SE was highlighted as a successful high-performance, high-participation company. L-SE has received many awards and much recognition, the most important coming from suppliers: Ford Motors' award rating of Q1 and General Motors' Targets for Excellence.

"We still have a long way to go," says Tinsley. An ongoing problem is communication—despite the 15-minute meetings at shift changes, 3-hour workshops held weekly, team meetings monthly to share business information, many committee meetings, daily morning meetings, and ad hoc meetings on special subjects.

"People get frustrated and angry because they want to be involved more, and people tend to question and criticize what they have not been part of. There's a tug between the small group—which feels that it should be able to move ahead and that it needs to implement rather urgently and quickly—and the entire group, which wants to be involved and knows that gain sharing depends on productivity and quality. The volume of issues is such that you could spend all your time communicating.

"It's also difficult to revitalize spirit and attitude. Off-site renewal sessions are one way to do that. One good thing that has remained the same is our sensitivity to customer issues and to quality. It took a lot of hard work to get there, and that focus remains."

Standing in good stead

Good problem-solving capabilities are essential, as is a strong belief in the L-SE culture. "You have to be able to just listen, and to give in at times," says Tinsley. "You have to ask, 'How important is this, *really*, to me and to L-SE that we do this my way? Can I live with something else?' Then you either fight for your view or you relinquish. Others can tell if you *really* believe in something and want it. And they reciprocate. You have to be able to sit and talk and be respectful."

Challenges remain, of course, both the challenges that arise internally and those imposed by the external environment. While the initial impetus and exhilaration of creating the company are now history, the real challenge is to keep the flame alive and to continue to innovate.

"We're still head and shoulders above all traditional organizations and many nontraditional ones. We have strong belief in what we do, and support from management and union leadership," says Tinsley.

"I still feel very fortunate to work here," says Zidek. "It is at times very wonderful and at times very frustrating. We will be okay for many years to come."

Location: Headquarters, Cleveland, Ohio.
                 11 major facilities, including sites in Germany and
                 Finland; field sales and service offices worldwide.

President and CEO: Cary J. Nolan.

People: 4,400 worldwide.

History: Founded in 1914 by James Picker; sold to CIT Financial
                 Corporation in 1958; sold to RCA in 1980; sold to GEC
                 Ltd. of Great Britain in 1981. From $650 million in
                 annual revenues in 1989, became $1 billion company
                 in 1994.

Business: Manufactures diagnostic imaging equipment for the
                 health-care industry (computer tomography, X-ray,
                 nuclear medicine, and magnetic resonance imaging);
                 distributes radiological supplies; and services
                 equipment installed worldwide.

                 Major joint ventures with: AT&T in lease financing,
                 Varian in radiation therapy, Marubeni and Shimadzu
                 in Japan, HCL in India, and GEC in Australia and France.

Sales: $1.003 billion.
                 R&D spending at 10.7% of equipment revenues;
                 capitalization at $339 million.

Commentary

Picker's implementation of Total Quality Management (TQM)
has been remarkable in several respects. First, it shows that a strong
focus on quality and customer satisfaction can unify a corporation's
culture. When he joined Picker as its CEO, Cary Nolan found a
patchwork of values and philosophies from several distinct periods in
Picker's history, and his experience had shown him a way to bring people
together through what Picker named Quality Driven Leadership.

Second, the most visible aspect of implementation is Picker's annual Qualithon, a day-long event where employee teams display their projects and vie for company awards. Picker approaches this type of event with more energy and consistency, and with more success, than any other organization we know of. Picker's Qualithon demonstrates a number of essential components of effective implementation, particularly recognition, communication, and top management's commitment to quality.

The third aspect is Picker's methodical benchmarking, using not one model but basing its process on three distinct models: IBM, Xerox, and the Malcolm Baldridge criteria. Picker's experience demonstrates how each of these models is particularly valuable in certain aspects of implementation and shows that all three models are essential in order to achieve all-around success. (It's also interesting that Picker views ISO 9000 as compatible with some aspects of TQM but not with others.)

Finally, Picker has an unusual visualization of the TQM model. It will be of particular interest to some readers, and it's worth getting the detailed diagrams and accompanying dialogue from Dr. Don Plante, Picker's Vice President of Quality and Technology.

—WINOC

When he arrived in 1989 as Picker's new CEO, Cary Nolan asked a particular question of many people in the organization: "What is Picker's culture?" He got so many different answers that he saw "a sharp need for a unifying culture," which he defines as a set of principles and beliefs that unify and guide the actions of employees.

"A lot of smart people were moving in a lot of different directions," he says. Most notably, there were the long-time employees who had the very family-oriented Picker culture from the 1960s and earlier; many line managers had come from General Electric; key financial managers had come from ITT; and people in sales had their own unique culture.

The existing culture was so fragmented that Nolan describes Picker in 1989 as "an organization with an identity crisis. If the culture favored any focus, it was technical. Engineering would develop a product and somebody else might or might not worry about dollars or about pleasing the customer. Something was needed that would enable Picker to benefit from both the academic and business disciplines."

Emphasizing that "we are all products of our environments," Nolan notes that he came to Picker from Xerox, where he'd had exposure to TQM, albeit "not all positive." He saw that quality could provide a focused culture and that total quality would force more attention to the customer.

"I made the commitment shortly after I arrived, in the course of reorganization. I got one of the intellectually smartest people on our staff, crowned him Vice President of Quality, and told him, 'I want you to work directly with me. You and I, along with a consultant, will form a program that we are most comfortable with, and we'll figure out a name for it.'"

How TQM changed culture

Picker named its process Quality Driven Leadership (QDL) and launched it in late 1990.

How has the culture changed? Dr. Don Plante, Vice President of Quality and Technology, sees a number of changes.

"First, the language has changed. People talk about improvement, not the status quo; about forming teams; and about quality.

"Second, teamwork is prevalent, and managers are supporting QDL. When I go to our annual quality fair, our Qualithon, I say to an exhibitor, 'That's a neat project. If Picker didn't have QDL, would you have done that anyhow? In the first year or so, only one out of three said yes.

'The others said, 'It never would have happened.' The response from those other two out of three was pretty evenly divided between, 'I can do it now because my manager supports it,' and 'I can do it now despite my manager.' Nowadays, however, managers are generally supportive because they have discovered that teamwork helps *them* succeed.

"A third change is measurement. Picker and its parent (General Electric Company of the United Kingdom—no relationship to General Electric of the U.S.) are very financially driven, with lots of financial measurements but with few nonfinancial ones.

"So we set up a corporate QDL Measurement Scorecard to track things such as customer and employee satisfaction, R&D effectiveness, and product quality. The CFO reports to senior staff on financial schedules and data, and I use the scorecard to report on nonfinancial data.

"A fourth change is that we have a lot more focus on the customer, a lot more zeal for the customer. We see that come through in business results. Our products have a lot of configurations. When a machine has 10,000 parts, and when the sales force sells that machine on the basis of its optimum performance, there's a lot that could fail."

In its focus on the customer, Picker was reorganized into strategic business units which cut across product lines. Picker defines quality as meeting customer requirements. Its guiding principles for QDL are: meeting customer requirements, total employee involvement, and continuous performance improvement.

In the course of its customer focus, Picker emphasized a broader definition of a customer (any person or team who receives your work output), what the customer's requirements are (we think we know but are often surprised), the capacity for negotiation (an amazing amount is negotiable, even with external customers), the need to increase a customer's expectations (above and beyond what the competition can deliver), and the need to deliver products and services that meet the customer's requirements (on time and right the first time).

Every employee has been taught a ten-step Continuous Quality Improvement Process, a quality tool that teaches employees how to satisfy customers.

Incidentally, creation of a common culture and focus on the customer were two of three fundamental strategies on which Nolan embarked. The third strategy is a focus on the top line—orders and revenues—instead of on the bottom line. The idea is to produce profits via growth.

At stage center: Qualithon

Improvement and teamwork are very much in evidence at the Qualithon, a one-company combination of a trade show and state fair. About 80 teams, including some from Picker locations around the world, set up displays to showcase accomplishments. Each team has planned and created an exhibit to show what that team did in the past year and to tell how that achievement has benefited Picker.

In the displays, the costumes, the VCR shows and other technical wizardry, and the popular themes (such as Jurassic Park), there is a strong current of salesmanship, and for good reason. Teams compete for the President's Award, which is awarded to the top two teams, winner and runner-up, that best exemplify the principles of QDL. The judges select the finalists, but Nolan personally picks the winners.

The Qualithon is visited by employees—all are invited to attend, and 1,200-1,500 do—as well as suppliers, customers, and even representatives of other companies contemplating their own quality fair.

Top management vigorously supports the Qualithon. "It has a fond place with me for a couple reasons," says Nolan, "especially because quality programs can be very nebulous. The Qualithon, however, is very tangible.

"People spend weeks and months preparing for it and executing it. Qualithon enables a lot of people to take on a role completely foreign to them—and to enjoy it immensely.

"Imagine if you were one of 200 employees in the finance department, and you hardly ever dealt with anyone outside your department. If you have an exhibit at the Qualithon, you are in effect a salesman, selling a product you are very proud of to a group of people you'd never see otherwise.

"I believe there's a salesperson hidden inside every one of us. We train our participants. We encourage them to make their exhibit fun and informative, to develop eye-catching graphics that present their story so a nonspecialist can understand it. The teams display amazing creativity in their presentations. Teams can and do include suppliers and customers."

Each Qualithon has a theme. A look at themes through the years reflects Picker's progressive journey in QDL. The first year's emphasis was on teams using the continuous quality improvement process or Picker's problem-solving process.

Year two focused on obtaining measurable results. Year three reflected Picker's entrance into the process management stage of QDL. Years four and five focused on measuring up to change in three ways: on becoming change agents within the company, on setting and achieving stretch goals, and on improvements that more directly benefit external customers.

Encouraging the spirit of the competition, Picker presents awards for the best booth design, the best team name, the zaniest team or booth, and the team with the most spirit.

But the most coveted honor is the President's Award, won by the best team. For example, in 1993 this award was won by a cross-functional team from Cleveland, "X-ray 81." This team, which had a supplier as a member, reduced costs 30% on installation and warranty for new equipment, for an annual savings of $148,000.

In 1995 the winning team's entry was a new process that reduced inventories—in raw materials, work-in-progress, and finished goods—by $7.3 million in just one year in one area: Magnetic Resonance

Imaging (MRI). The runner-up increased the life of CT tubes 25%, resulting in dramatically improved reliability for customers and $3 million in savings on warranty costs for Picker.

A simple three-level quality model

When Plante started his new career as Vice President of Quality and Technology, he had not heard of TQM. With a Ph.D. in system science, he says, "I needed to develop a system concept of how TQM would be deployed at Picker. Conceptually, QDL evolved into a very simple model. QDL seeks to make improvements at all three levels at which an organization performs: the work level, the business process level, and the organizational level. Basically, Picker has implemented QDL in three stages corresponding to those three levels.

"At the work level, products and services, called outputs, are created and problems are solved. At the business process level, outputs are linked together across the horizontal organization to deliver value to internal and external customers. At the organizational level, strategies, decisions, organizing, and planning occur.

"As we benchmarked various companies, we found that some were better than others at different levels, so we went with the best one in each case."

From Xerox: employee involvement

In its first stage at Picker, QDL took the form of a very comprehensive employee involvement program, improving performance at the work level. For this stage, Picker benchmarked Xerox's TQM process, Leadership Through Quality.

"Tackling the employee level first made a lot of sense because it would involve everyone," says Plante, "and we were out to change the company's culture. Emulating Xerox made a lot of sense because their TQM process was essentially an employee involvement program and because Mr. Nolan, being from Xerox, would be very comfortable leading a Xerox-like effort.

"So we hired a consulting firm that was a Xerox spin-off to help us get started, held a two-day kick-off workshop with senior staff to agree on about 30 elements of implementation and strategy, and proceeded to cascade quality training top-down throughout Picker.

"All employees were taught two quality tools. A 10-step Continuous Quality Improvement Process (CQIP), virtually identical to a Xerox tool, taught employees and work teams how to produce quality products and services. For the second tool, a 6-step Picker Problem-Solving Process (PPSP), we just called Xerox's 800 number and ordered their problem-solving manuals by the bushel. We left the Xerox name on the cover and added our QDL logo."

While benchmarking Xerox, Plante learned of some things the company wished it had done differently, and he incorporated these differences into QDL:

1. Participation on teams is mandatory; everyone needed for the team to succeed is assigned to the team by their managers.
2. Managers commission teams (rather than teams being formed at the discretion of employees); managers assign, empower them, and inspect their progress.
3. Involve union leadership early in the process (the Picker Solon facility is represented by the International Brotherhood of Electrical Workers Local #1370.
4. CQIP was taught first, before PPSP (rather than vice versa); Picker figured that its people already had problem-solving skills and that CQIP had the potential to stop problems from happening in the first place.

Early on, most teams were formed out of the workshops that taught the tools. Called QDL teams, they used either CQIP or PPSP to do their projects. By the end of QDL's second year, all employees had received training and over 500 QDL teams were commissioned.

Typically a team has 4-7 employees, tries to meet weekly for an hour to work on its project, and completes its project in 6-9 months. The number of QDL teams has held at the 500 level, although Picker has stopped counting. About 10% of these teams can point to savings in excess of $100,000.

Commenting on the success of Picker's teams, Plante says, "Our environment already was receptive to teams being formed to work on a problem."

From IBM: process improvement

As more teams formed, they became more cross-functional in nature and more likely to tackle multiple outputs, or strings of outputs—in other words, to seek to improve a business process.

Meanwhile, impending in a major Picker market was the European Community Medical Device Directive, which would require compliance with the ISO 9000 Quality Management System standard; this standard also focused highly on business processes.

So in year three Picker began the business process improvement stage of QDL, for which it benchmarked IBM.

"Cary and I visited Motorola to benchmark their Six-Sigma program, but we weren't ready for the measurement discipline it involved," says Plante. "Six-Sigma requires measurement of defects, and our workers were still fearful of what our managers might do with such data.

"On the other hand, IBM was more focused on cycle-time reduction and on analyzing how processes worked across the horizontal organization. That's what we needed because our sales and service channels were matrixed into our business units. So we launched stage two by flying the entire senior staff to Rochester, Minnesota, to benchmark IBM."

The IBM model defined a good process as effective (all outputs within it meet their requirements), efficient (which Picker defines as fast and accurate), adaptable (because things change), and under control (it behaves the way it was designed to behave). Processes should be flow-charted and analyzed for improvement.

"The transition to stage two," says Plante, "required us to marry the IBM approach to our measurement culture, our Xerox-based efforts, and ISO 9000. And we wanted to do it without adding more quality tools for employees to learn. So we defined a process to be improved as a special type of problem to be solved, and we applied PPSP to it in a prescribed manner.

"Picker is financially driven and has focused greatly on cost-reduction programs. So we were very careful not to talk about efficiency in the context of cost; even so, QDL has had to outlast and live down people's memories of the most recent of those cost-reduction programs.

"So we preached speed and accuracy. Having seen companies pursue one at the expense of the other, we knew we needed both speed and accuracy. We didn't want employees slowing down to get accuracy or rushing to get speed."

By emphasizing the mapping of business processes only from output to output to output, Picker also linked the Xerox-based CQIP tool with ISO 9000, which calls for procedures and work instructions. For Picker, strings of outputs became the basis for procedures; and CQIP done for individual outputs became the basis for work instructions. This had the added advantage of tailoring the ISO 9000 effort to the considerable size of Picker's organization; smaller organizations need fewer procedures.

Process improvement teams at Picker are called Process Management Teams to emphasize that improvements at the business process level are foremost a management responsibility. "After all," says Plante, "improving a business process can very well involve changing people's jobs and changing company policy and practices. Workers have neither the will nor the authority to do some of those things."

Picker's view of ISO 9000 is worth noting. "Given our efforts in employee empowerment, ISO 9000 could be viewed as somewhat of a setback at the worker level. It calls for a lot of procedures and documentation which are exactly the non-value-adding kinds of things that we hoped to eliminate through empowerment.

"But ISO 9000 coincided with our entry into stage two of QDL. When we tackled ISO 9000 certification, our view was that we were still in the very early stages of QDL, that ISO was a relatively low hurdle, and that it would advance us in the area of business process improvement."

QDL's business process stage started slowly.

"Mr. Nolan correctly sensed that the senior staff was not entirely on board with this, so he directed that every division start with one pilot process improvement project. This occurred in year three of QDL. Those first dozen projects quickly doubled, because everyone in the organization saw major opportunities for improvement once we got going—although most workers had already figured that out."

To the existing 500 QDL teams were added three to four dozen Process Management Teams, usually working on the subprocesses under their control. Several of these teams have been responsible for savings in excess of $1 million.

Year four continued with the theme of business process improvement, but with an emphasis on measurement, on refresher training, and on developing receptivity for making changes. All these were combined in the theme "measuring up," which extended through year five. Year five was transitional in nature.

"We tried to get management's attention on some of the misalignments that were creeping in. We were telling employees they were empowered, but too many of them saw their manager or supervisor as being a damn autocrat, micro-controlling every movement. We wanted to improve the accuracy of business processes, but employees were reluctant to measure defects for fear of what their manager would do with the data.

"We wanted to improve whole processes, even re-engineer them, but it was difficult to find managers who felt true ownership for those processes. We had involved managers in QDL from day one but, not surprisingly, by year six QDL was stalling, and managers were the culprits.

"The organizational level of performance was lagging. An example is the appraisal system. We had changed the culture to make continuous improvement the expected norm, yet the appraisal policy still said that plateaued performance was acceptable. So we got the appraisal system changed on paper, but in practice it still lags behind."

QDL had been espoused from the top; it now needed to be driven from the top to change from leadership-driven quality to quality-driven leadership. Plante says, "The time had come to flip QDL from being bottom-up implemented to being top-down implemented. And the mechanism to do that is Baldridge."

From Baldridge: doing it from the top

In year six Picker formally adopted the Malcolm Baldridge National Quality Award Criteria, which Nolan says will advance QDL to the next level. The Baldridge is Picker's way to focus on the third level of performance, the organizational level.

This third benchmark actually dovetails well with earlier efforts. Both Xerox and IBM Rochester have won the Baldridge Award. Also, Picker's QDL programs have been designed since inception to be compatible with the Baldridge criteria. For example, Picker's criteria for the President's Award in the Qualithon are Baldridge-based.

At his 1996 stakeholder meetings with employees, Nolan officially launched the third stage of QDL, saying, "After five years of effort, we have built the foundation and walls of our house of quality. We need a roof: we will pursue the Malcolm Baldridge Award in the five years ahead. Welcome to the second half of our pursuit of quality."

The pursuit of the Baldridge Award points up another crucial element to the success of QDL, namely the tenacity and vision of the two individuals at the top who personally champion the cause.

"World-renowned quality guru Dr. Deming states constancy of purpose as his first and most important point," says Plante. "In Mr. Nolan we have had that here at Picker.

"As for myself, I've had to be persistent. If I believe something in the existing system is wrong or incompatible with QDL principles, then I keep working to change it. It took several years to change the appraisal system. I proposed mandatory leadership training for three years before finally getting the order for it.

"In our very first QDL workshop for senior staff in 1990, we developed answers to about 30 strategic quality questions. Five questions were unanswered, and a couple were answered wrongly. I've pursued all of them, including the one that said we would not pursue the Malcolm Baldridge National Quality Award!"

PIONEER-STANDARD ELECTRONICS, INC.

Location: Headquarters, Cleveland.
                 53 U.S. branches; Canadian subsidiary.

President and CEO: James L. Bayman.

People: 2,000.

History: Created in 1963 as merger of Pioneer Electric Supply
                 (Cleveland, founded 1946) and Standard Radio (Dayton,
                 founded 1932).

                 In the mid-1960s the company had annual sales of $5
                 million. Half of that was in retail sales, which the
                 company eventually dropped; half was in industrial
                 sales, which did not even put the company in the top
                 100 electronics distributors.

                 The company has grown dramatically. In 1994 Pioneer
                 Standard reached the $1 billion mark and moved up to
                 rank third in an industry of 1,500 distributors serving
                 the $20 billion North American market.

                 Initial public offering in 1971. Acquisition of first foreign
                 subsidiary, Zentronics (Canada), in 1994.

Business: A distributor of industrial electronic components and
                 a systems integrator of computer products and
                 peripherals.

Sales: Combined sales of $1.3 billion.

Commentary

Pioneer-Standard is a textbook example of comprehensive planning activity, followed by rigorous implementation for outstanding results. Three decades ago the company had annual sales of $5 million. Its industrial sales did not even put the company in the top 100 electronics distributors. By 1996 it had climbed to third.

That type of growth is not realized by conducting business as usual. By dedicating intensive amounts of talent, energy, and dollars, Pioneer has made the leap to the next level by transforming its levels of customer service, its culture, and the way it does business.

Pioneer stock is an excellent performer: Pioneer has a history of outperforming its industry by 7%, and Pioneer's stock has done very well, whether evaluated over a period of 5, 10, or even 20 years. Pioneer is positioned well for the future. It has a strong management team, outstanding expertise and capability in engineering, and major customers who are industry leaders. The company has done very well in the marketplace.

Pioneer is also an outstanding example of total quality implementation throughout the entire organization. In the opinion of outside experts and top management inside Pioneer, there is a strong link between Pioneer's market performance and its quality culture.

—WINOC

To be seventh out of a field of 1,500 competitors is to rank in the top 1%. Pioneer-Standard wanted to do better than that. The challenge: if people in the company are already giving 100% effort, how can the company move up in the rankings?

When he became President in 1981, Jim Bayman's challenge was to continue to grow Pioneer, a company with a history of almost-constant growth and success. Pioneer grew with the total market for electronic components in North America. Like other distributors, Pioneer did not have a product of its own, but bought, warehoused, and sold suppliers' products.

Among Pioneer's customers are original equipment manufacturers of electronics products such as control systems, computers, modems, and medical diagnostic devices; industrial users of computer equipment; and value-added resellers, who write software products and configure computers. Pioneer added value by providing economies of scale, just-in-time delivery, and other services, and by eliminating redundancies between the manufacturer and Pioneer's customer.

An industry undergoing major changes

In the mid-1980s the electronic component and computer distribution industry underwent major changes. Commercial wholesale distributors and mass merchandisers suddenly began to carry some of the same products. Pioneer's customers wanted more competitive prices and more value-added services, particularly more comprehensive solutions to business problems.

It became clear to Pioneer's leadership that new approaches and solutions were needed. The old ways of building sales—adding staff, adding inventory, adding buildings—were not producing the expected results. "People were working very hard," says Bayman, "and coming to me to hire more people. We'd add five people, ten, or more, but we still couldn't leapfrog ahead."

Bayman discovered that his personal management techniques, the very ones that had enabled him to turn around Pioneer's Dayton operation, had ceased to serve him.

"With a business to turn around, my tendencies were perfectionist, and I was working very feverishly to make things happen. My team worked that way too until I realized we were physically headed for sheer exhaustion. Finally, we couldn't work any harder. We had to find a better way."

"We were no longer a small business," says Art Rhein, Senior Vice President, "where a manager can get results by sheer force of will. As a manager's span of control is diluted, the organization needs to develop a new dimension of management and to rely on the innate desire and ability of its people to do the right thing."

"So," says Bayman, "we stopped the world for an instant." That metaphorical instant came in 1989, when 25-30 senior managers from throughout the company met to craft Pioneer's vision and mission. Taking the lead with Bayman were two Senior Vice Presidents: Art Rhein, responsible for sales and marketing; and Janice Margheret, formerly of Ernst & Young, where Pioneer was one of her accounts.

"When we undertook this in 1989," says Margheret, "we were seventh in the industry. We asked, 'What's our vision of what we want Pioneer to be?' The answer was, 'to be the preferred strategic link between our suppliers and customers, in the top three independent distributors of electronic components and computer systems worldwide.' "

The mission statement says finally and emphatically, "We are committed to doing what we say we will do!"

In short, Pioneer committed itself to continued success and growth—and to a quality management culture where people would do the right thing, where processes would be streamlined, and where people would look for innovative ways to help customers solve problems and be successful.

Pioneer was determined to learn from the experience of other organizations going through the change process. Especially helpful would be Ernst & Young's experience and research; in turn, Ernst & Young's Center for Business Innovation published a Change Profile in 1995 that told Pioneer's success story.

Very early in the process a consultant came in to work with Pioneer's most innovative staff. He said, "I don't think your organization is ready for this, so before you re-engineer with all new automation and processes and procedures, I recommend you do some things in preparation." Those things were:

- Continuous Process Improvement (CPI), in which employees learned to work on small teams and solve problems;
- introduction of ISO 9000, which enabled Pioneer to achieve certification and to introduce quality on a manageable scale; and
- creation of a training infrastructure, including change management, which helps smooth the transition.

As is and to be

Next, Pioneer's people tackled Business Process Redesign: the creation of the Pioneer of the future. They had already looked at Pioneer as it existed at that point. They re-examined how Pioneer did things, looking at nearly every step and asking: "What can we eliminate? How could we redo this if we had our druthers?"

"Everybody had built little subprocesses," says Bayman. "We had never really pieced the organization together in detail. Our consultants made us think, with questions like, 'Why do you do that? Have you ever thought of doing this?' "

"We realized we couldn't flourish by operating according to our existing business assumptions," says Margheret. She recaps a few of the many outdated assumptions—paradigms which existed then and stood in the way of future success.

One paradigm: "Inventory has to be in all our locations to assure customers faster delivery." Today inventory is centralized in the Twinsburg distribution center, a fully automated operation that provides same-day shipment for orders received by 5 p.m.

Another: "We shouldn't show inside salespeople the cost of the product because they might lower the resale." This assumption prevented salespeople from booking an order when a call was made; they had to go to a product manager who basically told them what to say, and by the time they responded, the caller could have placed the order elsewhere. Ironically, inside salespeople were on 100% commission.

Another: "We can't buy inventory to a forecast because Sales would have us buy everything." In reality, Pioneer needed to be able to capture the forecast and figure what factors to use. This raised key questions: How should we forecast? Can we train existing staff to do the planning, or do we need new expertise?

Like other aspects of total quality management, Business Process Redesign is ongoing. "There will always be new data," says Bayman, "so we are continually modifying how we do business."

FutureStart™ is born

How could Pioneer make its mission come alive for its 2,000 people so they could help create the Pioneer of the future? How could Pioneer create the roadmap for its total quality improvement? As executive sponsor of the initiative, Margheret searched for the right word that everyone could rally around. She found it in FutureStart.

"The word indicates movement and vision, and the beginning of something that continues. It's about laying the foundation for something that will carry us for 15-25 years." Eleven initiatives were identified as essential to the implementation of FutureStart, each with its own tasks and requirements:
1. vision and planning,
2. performance measures,
3. communication,
4. training and development,
5. supplier management,
6. business process redesign,
7. quality management system,
8. continuous process improvement,
9. customer satisfaction,
10. reward and recognition, and
11. assessment and evaluation.

"It's important to emphasize that FutureStart isn't a program," says Margheret. "It will never stop. We call it an initiative or our lifetime journey.

"When we introduced FutureStart, we honestly thought it would take a few years, but we soon realized we're on this journey forever. This is so encompassing. First, all the elements cannot happen overnight. Also, when you're creating a new culture, it's very difficult to see the foundation being laid."

To help assure that FutureStart happens, Pioneer hired a Director of FutureStart to be responsible for its continued planning and communications. The company has made investments in training and development, quality operations, corporate communications, and software so that it can better plan and implement FutureStart.

Working off one plan

An element of success is that everyone at Pioneer works off one master plan. "We are pursuing an integrated plan that's full and comprehensive," says Margheret. "We have a whole change strategy. Communications and training are absolutely key to the success of FutureStart. If our people do not know about it and aren't equipped to implement it, total quality cannot happen.

"You can always communicate more. We use company E-mail, audiovisuals, newsletters, focus groups, and workshops to keep FutureStart in front of our people and to keep it vibrant. We highlight FutureStart in our annual reports, so the investment community is aware of our commitment to be more competitive and to increase customer satisfaction. We have a full-time corporate communications manager exclusively for FutureStart. You can never have enough communication."

Building in quality

"Pioneer started with the premise that it would use many of its own people and not add a lot of resources from outside," says Joe Creehan, Director of Quality. "It has been difficult because in effect people have one-and-a-half jobs.

"FutureStart is not a department, not a corporate program. It's an entire philosophy we have all committed to—not 10 or 20 or 100 of us, but the great majority of 2,000 employees at 53 locations across North America.

"Intensive improvement is part of everyone's job. For example, we didn't have a corporate person write our ISO 9000 manual. One of our branch managers and 6-8 salespeople did the documentation, developed a branch operations manual, and routed it to other branches for input. Finally, we sent the document to corporate headquarters to dot the i's and cross the t's."

Pioneer does have someone centrally responsible for many aspects of total quality, particularly in relation to ISO 9000 registration. Joe Creehan is an example of how Pioneer has groomed its own people to develop FutureStart. He joined Pioneer as MIS director and became involved in building the Twinsburg central distribution center, which boasts a totally computerized system. When Pioneer tackled ISO 9000, Jim Bayman said to Creehan, "You built Twinsburg on quality, so go make this happen."

"We started with ISO 9000," says Creehan, "because our people had already heard about it from our customers. The ISO certification process was a good way to continue to enlist our people in the entire quality process."

Most distributors do ISO certification only for their distribution center. Looking ahead to FutureStart, Pioneer also achieved ISO 9002 registration for sales, product management operations, systems integration, and connector- and cable-assembly operations—in short, all processes which come into direct contact with customers.

"We have standardized our processes, the way we do things," says Creehan. "That includes the process of defining and solving problems. A big cultural change has been the understanding of the concept of process. We realize that if we do the right process, the right thing, the first time, then the customer will be served. How do we maintain customer satisfaction? We measure processes. If we understand and fix the processes, and get to the root cause of problems, then customer satisfaction will be an automatic outgrowth.

"We gather corporate performance measures so people see that the company values quality. Top management must be interested in quality. They must understand that doing things right will produce results naturally. They must recognize individuals: Jim Bayman calls people to congratulate them on a success or to prod them on a problem.

"The only reason we do quality is to increase customer satisfaction and profits: to increase sales and reduce costs." Pioneer has issued a statement to its people on quality:

1. Meet or exceed customer expectations to increase revenue.
2. Do the right things the first time to reduce costs.
3. Everyone takes ownership. Everyone takes quality personally. It's not "someone else's" job.

"If you ask our people about quality," says Creehan, "anyone in the company should be able to feed those three points back. The large majority of our people have internalized them."

Training throughout

In the old Pioneer, training was limited to a few employees and a few topics. Today many more people are trained in many more things.

"Training is absolutely essential to our ability to progress and develop," says Margheret. "We took a complete university-style approach that parallels the prerequisites and progressive series of classes in formal education. We brought on talent to develop a curriculum architecture."

Professionals on staff have designed courses and an entire curriculum for each area in the company and every position. Employees know what they need for their particular job and for promotion. Training is performance-based, geared to changing behaviors and measuring ability. It includes self-paced instruction and is fully structured. Mentors monitor and test individual progress. Only when people can perform specified skills does Pioneer consider them trained.

"FutureStart is a global effort, a large change," says Margheret. "We are implementing many tools and processes, and training is the only way to get people comfortable and skilled." From a training staff of two in 1990, the department has grown to 15 people. The annual budget for training is $4 million, which encompasses everything except employee time spent in training.

Pioneer considers that figure to be on the minimal side and would like to be able to allocate more.

The architecture of the University of Pioneer focuses on two types of skills: on job-specific and technological skills, and on managerial and problem-solving skills. Courses progress from basic to complex.

New recruits in sales, for example, take courses in basic selling; advanced staff, who sell highly complex products, master solution-based selling and take courses with advanced technical content. All salespeople are required to understand the application of each part they sell and how it benefits the customer. Through training, salespeople use more automated tools and are familiar with constantly emerging new products.

The system works. Intel rated Pioneer #1 in technical sales accreditation and gave Pioneer a bonus.

"Training and development give Pioneer a foundation to attract and retain a highly qualified sales staff," says Margheret. "Vendors want to work with us because we are qualified to help customers. Customers want to work with us because we sell solutions. Nobody else is really doing this to the extent we do."

Selling solutions

Total quality has enabled Pioneer to give customers more value. "FutureStart has brought more of our people into the process of looking at a problem and finding better solutions," says Rhein. "A typical customer problem is forecasting business, and so customers place multiple orders and want faster delivery.

"In the past, our salespeople would call Materials and ask, 'What can you do to help?' Our first instinct was to increase our inventory to give customers a buffer against unpredicted demand.

"Today we send a cross-functional team—sales, materials management, MIS, and financial people—to examine the customer's problem from beginning to end. Maybe we can help them develop a better system by suggesting internal tools to better predict the demand frequency or by removing redundancy from their process to save time on certain steps. As a result, we find a better solution, reduce cost in the system, and gain new opportunities with that client."

A classic example of selling solutions is Pioneer's work with a major manufacturer of medical diagnostic equipment. This customer sells machines that analyze blood; the machine has a computer system that produces diagnostic readouts, and Pioneer provides the integrated computer system.

"This customer used to build its own PCs," says Margheret. "We proposed to them: 'Your core competency is building blood analyzers and producing reagents, not building PC systems. Our core competency is building computer systems. We'll design and build your system to your specifications, load your software, and ship your product to your customers.' Our customer said, 'We thought you just supplied parts.' We responded with an invitation to see our ISO-certified integration center.

"We have to understand each customer's needs. This customer requires services such as computer-to-computer linkage. We said we'd do that. Their products require FDA approval, which involves a different level of quality from what we had done. We said we'd learn and do that. As a result, Pioneer is the only distributor to win this customer's Supplier of the Year award five years in a row. Today this customer is in Pioneer's top ten customers. To provide solutions, we look beyond the nine dots," says Margheret, referring to the puzzle which must be solved by going outside assumed and conventional boundaries.

This success story didn't happen quickly or easily. Before it could happen, top management had to envision it, prepare the organization to deliver it, and invest considerable resources with the expectation of ultimate success.

"It took six months to design our process to the stage of presenting our proposal to this customer," says Margheret, "and another six months to our first shipment. In that year we were spending investment dollars: all this in a culture where for years our people focused simply on booking the customer's order and getting the check, and where the customer said, 'If I wanted it tomorrow, I'd ask for it tomorrow.' "

Implementing change

Bayman describes the cultural transition as a migration from supervision, which says, "I'll tell you what to do," to management, which says, "Give me a report on what you did," and ultimately to leadership, which focuses on the future and says, "Keep me posted and keep up the good work." The old attitude, he says, was that working equaled doing; the new attitude is that working equals accomplishing.

"We had to work smarter," says Bayman, "to achieve positive results through positive techniques and through our people. My biggest problem was learning how to manage myself. I had to develop a tolerance for people making mistakes. We had to teach people to think, to have confidence.

"We hire capable people and train them to make commitments on our behalf and to fulfill those commitments. We deal with very high-tech products that have a high rate of obsolescence and a very short life cycle. This business is incredibly people-oriented and people-intensive. Pay and benefits account for 70 cents of every dollar spent. Our differential is how our people interface with our customers. Does everyone live the mission day by day, minute by minute?"

The change at Pioneer was manifested in many ways. For example, for years, people needed to secure approval for suppliers' orders over $50. The magic number was notched up, first to $100, and eventually to $1,000.

Managers have learned new skills: the ability to be a better coach and mentor. Pioneer leadership works to tap into managers' native talents to be innovative thinkers and to spend more time developing their people rather than monitoring and policing.

"We had consultants come in," says Rhein, "to advise and help create an environment that walks the talk and that helps managers shed the feeling that they need to know all, see all, and decide all.

"Managers are very conscious of the subtle messages we send. For example, if a branch manager has a problem and can't reach his immediate supervisor, we encourage him to contact whoever can help get the job done. As the supervisor, we shouldn't feel uncomfortable, let alone threatened, because we don't know what's happening. You have to be secure to do this. Managers need to have a high degree of trust and predictability with each other and with senior management."

"Tremendous change is very difficult," says Bayman, "but our leaders realize we have an immense moral responsibility to deliver. We have accelerated empowerment throughout the organization. Giving it to people is one thing; their accepting it is quite another.

"We have incentives—personal rewards and public acknowledgment—and constant positive reinforcement. Pay is tied into articulated goals and results. Pioneer has a history of paying for results. Most people do want to be paid fairly and to give fair return."

Focus on four fronts

Who is Pioneer's constituency? Today Pioneer sees four groups as prime customers: in addition to literal customers, they are suppliers, employees, and shareholders.

"Each of those has various needs and desires," says Margheret, "and FutureStart enables us to accomplish all those needs for all four groups. Pioneer grew up being very supplier-centric because our product was totally the supplier's product.

"Now we have a much more balanced mobile: we know that if we can solve problems for customers, we will be very attractive to suppliers, and if we satisfy our employees, they will serve our customers. The final result is better value for shareholders."

Bayman sees this balance as essential to Pioneer's continued growth. Suppliers want the distribution channel that's easiest to do business with and to convey their product to the user. Employees want to work for the company with the best tools so they have maximum ability to satisfy customers and to prosper. And customers want to buy economically from a hassle-free supplier.

"Big distributors have a greater ability to design the infrastructure to accomplish all this and to design programs to satisfy those three constituencies: to attract employees, get franchises to work with suppliers, and get more customer business."

Success by many criteria

For eight consecutive years, Pioneer-Standard has set sales records; sales have increased 22 of the 23 years the company has been public. Here are some other signs of success:

- Since 1992 the company has received more than 50 awards from companies it works with—20 awards in 1995 alone.
- Net income has shown dramatic gains in 1991, 1993, and 1994; in 1994, up 35% from 1993.
- The P/E multiple is 40x, compared to multiples of 8-17 for its nearest three competitors.
- Stock has split four times between 1991 and 1995.

Since 1992 Pioneer has graded its performance by having WINOC perform an assessment using the criteria established for the Malcolm Baldridge National Quality Award. Over four years, Pioneer has shown a 136% rate of improvement, and its 1995 score was the highest of more than 100 assessments performed by WINOC. Typically, after companies achieve early successes, the rate of progress slows because scores at higher levels are more difficult to improve. What is especially remarkable about Pioneer, however, is its continued high rate of progress, which indicates success in tackling progressively more complex and difficult issues.

Bayman sees continued growth as the challenge of the future: growth within the company as well as through further acquisitions. "We will change through acquisitions worldwide. We will also make strategic changes in the business, such as removing even more redundant costs. All of us—our people, our customers and vendors, our shareholders—will continue to prosper. Our vision is to be a $3.5 billion company by the year 2000."

REPUBLIC ENGINEERED STEELS, INC.

Location: Headquarters in Massillon, Ohio.
Ten operating facilities in six states (Ohio, Pennsylvania, Indiana, Illinois, Connecticut, and Maryland).

Chairman and CEO: Russell W. Maier.

People: 4,500.

History: Created as an employee-owned company in November, 1989, with the purchase of LTV Steel's Bar Division. Roots date back to 1886, when the company began as Berger Manufacturing Company, in Canton, Ohio. In 1930, after a number of mergers, it became part of Republic Steel; in 1984 Republic Steel merged with Jones & Laughlin to form LTV Steel, the second-largest U.S. steel maker.

Plants vary tremendously. They range in size from as few as 30 employees to as many as 2,000. The oldest plant is 103 years old; the newest, a state-of-the-art facility in Canton, links five separate steel-making steps into a single process.

Major awards include U.S. Department of Labor LIFT award, three General Motors Mark of Excellence awards, four Ford Q1 awards, and Honda Production Support Award.

Business: Leading U.S. producer of high-quality bar and specialty steels engineered for the most demanding applications; products include carbon, alloy, stainless, tool, and specialty steels produced as bar products in the hot-rolled, cold-finished, and forged condition. Major markets are automotive, parts suppliers, forgers, bearings, aircraft, off-highway, and service centers.

Sales: $805 million (shipments of 1 million tons).

Commentary

The ultimate in ownership is a company which has been purchased by its employees. Cooperation and participation take on new meaning when the people who do the work also share in major decisions about the company—and own it.

The people of Republic Engineered Steels have come a long way since the day they learned that their parent, LTV Steel, was going to shed them. After working hard and waiting for a buyer to materialize, the employees bought the company through an Employee Stock Ownership Plan (ESOP).

A well-crafted governance system is but one of the important components in this success story. Considerable resources have been devoted to educating employees so they can function as informed shareholders. In the first four years of ESOP education, the company spent $4.2 million on a program that equips all employees to read shareholder information, understand how the company is run, and make decisions within the context of the company's business, its competition, and its environment.

When the employees bought the company, they invested $20 million of their own money, an average individual investment of $4,000. As employee owners, they have been successful. Despite being in a highly competitive and mature industry, Republic Engineered Steels has invested more than $250 million in its facilities and has added new plants.

—WINOC

It was the fall of 1986, and the Bar Division of LTV Steel had had its share of the tough times faced by American steel companies— competing with new technology abroad, seeing steel prices drop faster than the company could take costs out, and reducing the workforce from 20,000 to 5,000.

At that point LTV told Russell Maier, the President of the Bar Division, that LTV was going to exit bankruptcy—but without his division. It might be closed or sold.

"What does it mean?" Maier's people asked when he told them the news. He didn't know. He said he didn't think it meant anything *good*.

"They can't do that—*can* they?" Yes, they could. "What's going to happen?"

"I don't know what will happen," Maier told them, "but I do know one thing: if we can create something of value, if our customers perceive that we provide value and a product they want, and if we create a positive cash flow, somebody *will* want this company."

The Bar Division had lost $100 million in 1986. "We met with our people to review our financial statement and our strategies. People responded by working hard to turn things around. The good news was that in two years, by the end of 1988, we were in the black, a salable asset. The bad news was that potential buyers were few, and unlikely to reinvest in the business."

Found: a buyer—the employees

In the meantime United Steel Workers of America Local #1200 had hired its own investment banker, who recommended that the employees buy the company through an Employee Stock Ownership Plan (ESOP).

"The advantage of an ESOP is that employees who are shareholders have a greater stake in the company. Being employees as well as shareholders, they will wait longer for return on their money. And they will be willing to let the cash flow back into the business to enhance the longer-term profitability of the company."

After a number of meetings, management agreed to join with the union and attempt to structure the purchase.

"And so," says Maier, "it became apparent that the somebody who wanted the bar division business was *us*: 5,000 employees invested $20 million. The average individual investment was $4,000. A preferred stock plan was created for the benefit of the employee-owners at the time of the investment."

The first major hurdle was to pull everything together: to negotiate the purchase and to secure the approval of bankruptcy court. In November, 1989 (three years after LTV had announced its decision to shed the bar division) everything came together, and Republic Engineered Steels was born with the union's real urging and total support.

When employees are the owners

Union and management arrived at a governance system that was balanced in a number of important ways. It balanced the needs of the company and of employees as individuals. The board of directors had a balance of management and union representation: four seats for steelworkers, three of them elected from the plant floor, and four seats for management, one of them Maier's.

"Cooperation and participation are embedded in the contract language, in everything we do. We have tried to push it to every level in the company: from the board level to the plants and into every department and crew. Our people have to be able to make tough decisions for the company, and they have to be committed to reinvest in the business. An ESOP is financially the right structure for encouraging employees to make the right decisions. It offers employees an opportunity to share in the company's financial success as reflected in the value of their stock."

Corporate ownership was a new universe for employees. It raised questions such as, "Do you pay me more in wages or do you reinvest in the business?" and "Can I fire the foreman?"

"Whatever area you work in this company," Maier told employees, "You will have the definite ability to affect the outcome of the business."

And so the employees bought the company. But there was little time to celebrate. Republic had been part of the 1980s' highly leveraged buyouts, yet within a year of its formation it was part of the 1991 auto recession, along with its leading customers.

"We got through that period because we relied on the cooperation and participation of our employees," says Maier. "At one point I implied that one way out might be that we cut employment. That didn't sell so well, so I came back and said, 'Okay, we'll cut costs instead, and all employees will work on it because we have to do it.' Employees really cared, and they responded with lots of ideas. In 18 months participative teams cut another $40 million more out of the cost of doing business.

"Ultimately, of course, we had to invest in new technology and equipment. By 1993 we were out of the recession and had been able to pay down significant amounts of debt while restructuring our original loan so that we could reinvest. Since we began in 1989, we've been able to make capital investments in excess of $250 million in our facilities, purchase and start up two new plants, sell $275 million of public bonds, and do an initial public offering of common stock.

"The ESOP was in everybody's best interest. It formed the foundation of today's efforts at joint partnership. We created the expectation that information will be available to everyone regarding the company's performance."

ESOP education key to success

A unique strength of Republic's ESOP is the education program that was created in 1990. "People felt the need to get a better and broader understanding of ESOP and what it meant. This is education," stresses Maier, "not work-related training."

Because employees were owners, Republic started to give them the type of information that all shareholders get, such as earnings statements and balance sheets. Soon employees responded, "For 40 years you didn't give us any information. You didn't even tell us anything. Now you give us all this. We don't know how to interpret it." That provided a great opportunity for labor and management to come together and put together an education program, which started in July, 1990. In the first four years, the company spent $4.2 million on ESOP education.

A one-hour course is offered approximately every two months to all employees. A sampling of topics: introduction to common stock ownership, understanding Republic's statement of income, the preferred stock plan, understanding Republic's balance sheet, competition in the bar steel industry, stock ownership benefits, the defined contribution plan, Republic's business plan, employee ownership in America, and how we compare.

The education program was developed in consultation with Kent State University's Northeast Ohio Employee Ownership Center, which trained a core group of 50 Republic people, both hourly and salaried, to teach the courses.

"This education gives Republic a very strong advantage. The more our people understand about this company and about business, the more intelligent the decisions they make on the floor. That education has turned out to be very powerful, especially in a larger company."

Management's biggest problem, believes Maier, is the widespread employee conviction that there is a clandestine operation behind the operation, a view summed up by the persistent belief that companies have two sets of books.

"The greater the information vacuum in a company, the greater the chance for inaccurate rumors. We just keep bombarding our people with facts, because we believe in empowering our people with facts. We still have rumors, and every day there are some pockets of employees who revert to the old beliefs and behavior, but at the end of the day most people believe they can find out the facts, so they can respond to rumors by saying, 'Charlie, it isn't that way.' "

ESOP: a new way of doing business

Dick Davis, a Vice President of the United Steel Workers of America, has worked with the four local unions at Republic (#1200, #1124, #1566, and #2327) from the very beginning. "We helped engineer a structure for employees to purchase and manage their own company," says Davis. "These plants are fascinating, and our union members in them are fascinating. They are part of a culture with a hostile and violent history, and it's amazing to watch this transition happen in a smart, practical way.

"A 60-year-old steelworker told me, 'I was really looking forward to my retirement, but for the first time in a 38-year career, I'm changing where I work. I've got an opportunity to make it different and better and more satisfying. So I think I'll hang around a few more years.' I find it fascinating how people are taking pride in being able to change a system or process or procedure that frustrated them for years but there wasn't any mechanism to change it.

"The participation goes literally from board of directors to shop floor. Facilities are run by decision-making, data-sharing. Decisions are made jointly, equally, based on the same information, and on all the information.

"An important piece of that is the creation of a sense of employment security and opportunity rather than a sense of threat coming from changes in technology and improved productivity. The agreement specifies that there will be no layoffs as the result of changes to better and more efficient systems. Instead, we are jointly responsible for finding alternative ways of training and using people.

"Union leaders, at these plants and at the international level, found it quite novel to be involved in a process of sharing in decision-making, of becoming proactive rather than reactive to the acts of management. Structured partnership is part of our collective bargaining agreement. It's institutionalized. Our people take a lot of pride in the company because they are owners *and* because they are proud of how it operates. I believe we're learning to do it better," concludes Davis.

Impact of ESOP

"The big difference in managing an ESOP is time," says Maier. "It takes much more time to do process. Everybody is informed and has the opportunity to present issues and contribute input. Our goal is to enable people with experience and expertise in a given subject to participate and provide input; management listens to the input, makes the decision, and communicates it to all."

The chief problem, for an ESOP or any company, says Maier, "is quite simply that our world changes every day, and we have to be constantly willing to change if we want to be in shape to compete. It's not easier in an ESOP; it may be harder, because it takes more time to inform and involve every level, from the board of directors to each plant and each department.

"This business is really complex compared to what it was 25 years ago, and there isn't any magic formula. As recently as a decade ago, you could hire someone with minimal skills and a strong back. At our newly opened state-of-the-art facility in Canton, the entry-level position requires the equivalent of a two-year technical-school education. To open that plant, Republic invested $7 million in technical training for about 125 employees, including training on the equipment at our supplier's plant in Italy.

"The only given in this business is that if you don't change, you will fail. That's not a comfortable thought, so I talk about it all the time. We need to make change a positive, to make change work for us, to achieve more flexibility in the way we do our work."

Growth industries, Maier points out, have an advantage: growth covers a lot of sins. In a mature industry like steel, companies are constantly under pressure to provide more value at less cost. "No matter how well we did it yesterday, we have to do it better today. There's always the pressure to tear it apart and do it all over again— and again. That's definitely not a natural habit for us in America. We need to find enjoyment in the *process* of improvement, not in the improvement itself."

Successes

Republic has, of course, done much more than be an ESOP and educate its people to become effective employee-owners. It has made real strides as an ESOP. In addition to significant financial restructuring and growth in value-added products, Republic has constructed a new steel making facility, the only one of its kind in North America.

Republic has improved quality performance. Defects, for example, have been reduced from 22 per million in 1992, "a pretty high number," to 1-2 per million. Customers expect Republic's products to work right the first time. As evidence of that fact, in 1993 Republic received Honda's Production Support Award for achieving zero defects and 100% reliability.

Cost-cutting measures have been implemented throughout Republic's plants. Measures range from recycling process water to the handling of raw materials. The biggest single measure to date saves almost $3.6 million per year by separating scrap steel for more efficient recycling.

"We are also constantly striving to produce steel with less mass, so it will be more fuel-efficient," says Maier. "If we don't, then the companies that make plastics or aluminum or composite products will."

The labor agreement specifies that pay raises are given on the basis of how fast employees take costs out of the system. When a plateau is reached, everybody gets a raise.

The good news today is that Republic Engineered Steels is reclaiming important markets. The scene has changed dramatically since the 1980s, when half of Maier's forging customers went out of business. Today the U.S. manufacturing base is growing, and Republic's U.S. customers export their products to Germany, Japan, and other overseas customers.

"All ESOPs, including Republic, are faced with a financial liability to repurchase employees' stock when they leave the company unless a public market exists for them to sell in. In 1995 we decided the right thing to do was to offer some stock to the public. Our charter required us to get a 72.5% shareholder vote. We got 80% approval because everyone understood how an initial public offering served their best interest. Because Republic used much of the proceeds from the stock offering to buy back employees' preferred stock, employees received $10,000 on that average initial investment of $4,000."

ESOP and the challenge of change

What is the biggest obstacle Republic faces? "The most frustrating thing is our inability to change fast enough, to knock down the old structure." Maier is referring not to the 50-year-old plants, as much as Republic would like to replace them, but to work practices and the ways people go about doing things.

"Over many years we—management and union—created a system that institutionalized certain practices: reward seniority, protect your own domain. One of the greatest changes we need, of course, is to operate by working together cooperatively. Putting income at risk is a foreign concept for our workforce.

"Hopefully, all of our people have gained a greater understanding of what an ESOP is. But even some of the people who do understand the need for change have a tough time when it affects them personally: 'Yes, Russ, I know we have to change, but not on my shift—wait a couple years until I retire.'

"All this is human nature and predictable. When we started, I hoped we could make the transition in six or seven years. Today I'd say I think it's going to take ten years. We just have to stay the course, and be consistent long enough. At Republic we clearly have the ability to solve our problems. All possibilities are still ahead—and a lot of hard work.

"Having said all that, I believe one absolutely true and most encouraging thing: once you get a new work system where you empower employees to work in self-directed teams, where employees have a say in governance, and where pay is linked to skills instead of to years of service, I've never seen a worker who gave it a legitimate chance who wanted to go back to the old system where he had to wait for someone to leave or retire in order to improve his destiny. Here employees are empowered to take greater control of their destiny and their own net worth."

REXROTH MOBILE HYDRAULICS

Location: Wooster, Ohio.

Vice President, Operations: Keith Homan.
Vice President, Sales and Administration: Mike Bickel.

People: 540.

History: Founded in 1952 as the Wooster Division of Borg-Warner. The plant first produced gear-type fuel and hydraulic pumps for jet and reciprocal-engine aircraft. In 1956 the plant switched to farm and industrial applications, and soon after it expanded to perform close-tolerance machining.

In 1979 this division became part of Rexroth Corporation, USA, which is based in Bethlehem, PA. Rexroth is a subsidiary of Mannesmann Rexroth of Germany, the world's largest manufacturer of hydraulic components and systems. The parent company, Mannesmann AG, also owns Mannesmann Demag.

Business: Manufactures hydraulic valves for off-road vehicles in agriculture, light manufacturing, mining, and forestry; also manufactures pumps and motors for 400 industrial applications; in 1994, added a line of piston pumps for the automotive market.

Offers wide range of specific products and custom options. Product specifications range widely in volume (1 to 2,000 gpm) or pressure (200 to 6,000 psi). Products are machined to very close tolerances, to a thousandth or millionth of an inch. The division markets products and systems from eight Rexroth facilities around the world.

Sales: $121 million.

Commentary

When talking to companies about pursuing ISO 9000 certification, we frequently hear someone say, "That wouldn't be possible for us. Our process is just too complex." To put that myth to rest, we present the Rexroth story, which is informative for all organizations, complex or not.

Companies don't get much more complicated than Rexroth Mobile Hydraulics, which has a high-precision manufacturing process that routinely measures parts to a millionth of an inch. To further complicate implementation of ISO, Rexroth's products are built in a wide array of customized options.

Rexroth has been very, very successful in its implementation of ISO 9000. Not only did Rexroth achieve certification on the first try and within 14 months, but it did so while introducing a major new product line.

Especially key to this success is the fact that Rexroth set ISO certification as a priority from the top. There was never a question of whether to pursue ISO; the only question was how long it would take. Rexroth is part of Mannesmann, an international leader in manufacturing, who sent the directive to Rexroth to obtain ISO certification. Over a two-year period, we saw how local leadership became very focused on ISO, dedicated resources to it, and conveyed its determination to employees, who carried out the implementation.

—WINOC

When Dick Greenham learned that Rexroth would be pursuing ISO certification, his response was, "Great!" As Quality Assurance Manager, Greenham had been responsible for seeing that Rexroth met the quality standards required by its customers and its customers' customers. Each market had its standards: there was Ford's Q1, GM's Targets for Excellence, and many others.

Many of these standards focused on product quality control in a narrow sense, that is, inspection by the Quality Department. Others looked at quality and at the business in a much broader context. In some cases, Rexroth was able to satisfy the standards easily; others were more difficult.

"We were satisfying all these systems, so when we learned that ISO involved satisfying just *one* system, we said 'Great!' We were not fearful. It was very attractive."

The product

Rexroth manufactures hydraulic valves for off-road vehicles in agriculture, light manufacturing, mining, construction, and forestry; it also produces pumps and motors for some 400 industrial applications; and in 1994 it added a third line of products, piston pumps for the automotive market.

In this industry it's not unusual for a company to carve a small niche, very dependably doing one size product, and only that. Rexroth, on the other hand, produces valves and pumps in a product line ranging in volume from less than 1 gallon to 200 gallons per minute and ranging in pressure from 200 to 6,000 psi or more.

Starting from a basic product line, Rexroth designs a system for each customer's needs. The line of pumps is extensive, with 450 different pumps; the line of valves offers customers 140 customized options.

"In the past," says Greenham, "a valve would have one to four sections, and we offered the customer a dozen options for those sections. As more and more requirements were made of valve performance, we added more customized options. We now have valves with nine sections, and customized options have increased to 140. It seems that every week we add another option."

Rexroth machines its products to very close tolerances: a thousandth of an inch is routine; even a millionth of an inch is fairly common. "Considerable engineering time and effort are expended to assure that a valve or pump will do what we say it will. We have to maintain control of extremely close tolerances. That requires a very skilled machinist, which in turn requires major training programs." All these elements compound the complexity of Rexroth's manufacturing process.

Every product is tested 100% in a simulation of its application. The test area for valves, for example, has 300 different test specifications. The test station is computerized: the product's identifying number is entered, and the machine automatically does the right tests in the right sequence.

ISO was inevitable

ISO certification was inevitable, says Keith Homan, Vice President of Operations, who has been with the company since 1976. Rexroth's parent, Mannesmann, is one of the world's 50 largest industries, and its U.S. divisions represent $2.5 billion in annual sales.

"Mannesmann is a major player in the European community, where the impetus for ISO originated. Mannesmann has operations and sales all over the world, so ISO certification is a big selling point. As for us here in Ohio, we import a lot of components from Rexroth locations around the world, and we sell our products worldwide."

Apart from that, Homan points out that the implementation of ISO has intrinsic value. "I saw that going through the exercise imposed by ISO would bring disciplines into this plant that we didn't have before. In an older company like ours, a lot of what you do just builds up over the years and doesn't get documented.

"We explored different ways of implementing ISO and decided to join WINOC's consortium instead of hiring a consultant. Besides being less expensive, this gave us the opportunity to mix with noncompeting companies, to work together, and to benefit from their viewpoints and experiences."

Rexroth also investigated a number of ISO registrars, looking for a good fit with the company. Rexroth chose its registrar on two main counts: for its premier reputation, which is respected by Rexroth's customers internationally; and for its capability to work with the company on its next round of certification, the automotive industry's QS 9000, which Rexroth will achieve by the end of the fourth quarter of 1997.

ISO implementation happened to coincide with Rexroth's addition of a third product line, a piston pump that is a high-volume product for the automotive industry. The line involved five years of work with the customer as well as with engineering personnel at the Wooster plant and in Germany.

"When you hire 200 new people *and* start ISO implementation, you know there will be problems," says Homan. "We have an ISO Steering Committee that includes myself; Mike Bickel, Vice President, Sales and Administration; Dick Greenham; Dan Brown, Quality Engineer; and Glenn Kaser, Union President, United Auto Workers Local #1239.

"The union knew our ISO goals and took part in the consortium and all other implementation activities. The Steering Committee knew and selected the individuals best suited for training. Our union members saw ISO as a job-security issue, as part of satisfying the customer, and they have given ISO good support."

Implementation

ISO demands that a company document everything it does *and* that the company prove it really does what it says it does. The concept is elegantly simple, but execution requires much time and energy.

"An essential key to the success of Rexroth's implementation was the decision to involve the people who actually do the work," says Dan Brown. He serves as Rexroth's ISO management rep, or ISO coordinator, and has been with Rexroth since October, 1994, when implementation began.

"We picked people from each department to write their own procedures," says Brown. "That gave employees ownership in ISO. They also had the chance to change things. We made a conscious decision when we told employees, 'Nobody knows better than you what it is you do. And if you see a flaw in the system, you have the ability to make the system better.'

"Also, a number of college students were hired the summer of 1995 to get this information onto paper in rough draft form. They had no preconceived notion of what people's jobs involved or should involve. Their rough drafts were given to manufacturing engineers, who asked, 'If that's what they're doing on that job, is it right? Do they have the best tool for the job?' Department heads held meetings to get input from all people on all shifts. 'This is what's written down. Is it correct?' Each department had to reach agreement.

"Rexroth initially had work procedures called routings. A routing, for example, would tell how we assemble a pump. When the college students had obtained their input from the people doing the work, we found that in many cases, people weren't following the routings. That raised the question, 'Is what they're actually doing a better way?'"

When the procedures were decided, Brown revised them into one readable collection, the ISO quality procedure manual.

"We sought out volunteers to write the procedures. Later, we turned our authors into our internal auditors. It's a natural progression, because they are familiar with the requirements of ISO specifications." After training, auditors are sent to departments other than their own, where they ask, "Are people in this department doing what is written down? Are they doing what they said they do?"

The challenges

"We knew that few companies succeed the first time out, and we also knew that few companies do it in 12 to 18 months," says Greenham. "We said, 'Yes, we can do that.' We motivated ourselves with one common goal. ISO got a lot of people motivated. And we were under deadline—the assessor was coming in December, 1995."

The biggest complication was for people to take time from their everyday routine—time to write the procedures, time to work on a team trying to resolve an issue, time for internal auditors to do their audits.

"The order," says Greenham, "came down from the Steering Committee as an edict: 'Do it.' Knowing that management is behind you and working with you makes it that much easier. People said, 'We can't do ISO and keep up with our normal jobs.' Keith Homan responded by saying, 'You don't make a choice between your job and ISO. ISO isn't something over and above your job. ISO is part of the job; it's how you do your job.'"

"I was very fortunate with auditors and procedure writers," says Brown. "A lot of people worked a lot of extra time for several months."

"We told people that ISO is a very important part of our goals, thus it must be done," says Homan. "And it had to be done by people inside the organization who know our business. New employees or outsiders couldn't do it."

Documentation wasn't always easy. Sometimes it involved fundamental changes. Each procedure had to be written so everyone could follow it uniformly. Before ISO implementation, each discipline at Rexroth had its own procedures: marketing and sales, design, engineering, manufacturing. Besides having different procedures, one discipline often didn't realize what the other disciplines were doing. Overcoming that lack of knowledge and independent approach wasn't easy.

Many benefits of ISO

Rexroth's people have seen many benefits resulting from the implementation of ISO.

In and of itself, says Greenham, "ISO is a good basic way to do business. Certain regimented things have to be done in order to manufacture a quality product. Some of our systems already had the element of continuous improvement. We always dealt with the leading edge of technology, but now we do it in a much broader way. Today, with ISO we apply continuous improvement to all areas. It involves, for example, secretaries asking, 'How do I do my job better?' as well as machinists measuring tolerances in millionths of an inch.

"ISO has also helped us get around problems that involved a lot of time and effort but that are really simple now that ISO's in place. Before, a customer reorder could involve digging up information from the previous order and refiguring the process. Now we can simply do it the same way again and again.

"We don't have to start over. We have documented the setup, machining, inspection, assembly, and even packing and shipping. Documentation benefits the customer and us. We know the process and the product were acceptable before, and we know the customer will get the exact same product."

Another benefit: Rexroth used to look at scrap cost. Now people look at that cost *and* at the reasons for the cost. Preventive action is taken. Yet another benefit is the sense of ownership among employees. "When we first told employees that procedures had to be written, there was initial opposition," says Brown. "People said, 'We've never had to write this down for 20 years.' But very quickly people saw the benefits.

"They saw how this saved time and labor by not having to reinvent things. People also saw they could change things to make them flow better—those little tiny things that make a job so much better. And people began to realize that as a team they can spend a certain amount of money to design and buy equipment and to improve procedures."

Another benefit is that Rexroth is scrutinizing customer satisfaction much more closely. "We've always considered ourselves customer-oriented," says Greenham. "ISO in effect said, 'If you say you're customer-oriented, show what you do to satisfy the customer. And by the way, what exactly does the customer want?' We have started to think through that systematically, to measure it, and to really look at it."

"Probably the most beneficial thing," says Brown, "is that we got to understand more about other disciplines. We have moved away from thinking as a department to thinking about how departments work with each other and have an effect on each other.

"For example, if marketing and design people are both working on the same thing, it makes sense to split the task and streamline it. People now understand other disciplines and have a better appreciation of how their job fits in the total picture. We have omitted overlapping, duplicative efforts. That pays off significantly. As an organization we pull together more."

Another benefit, says Homan, is a more disciplined approach in releasing new products, in the Failure Mode Evaluation and Analysis (FMEA). "At the design stage, we ask a number of questions. What can go wrong? What would happen if it did? Is it important? If so, what have we done to assure that won't go wrong? Next, in the process stage, we scrutinize all the details of manufacturing in the context of those questions.

"Both we and our customers are following these procedures in ways we would not have done before ISO. We are building quality and reliability into the product at a very early stage rather than waiting until the production phase.

"If you see ISO in the context of continuous improvement, then education of the workforce becomes an important part of it because the workforce doesn't come to us fully trained.

"We now have people who are better trained and better equipped to face the challenges. ISO isn't about putting a plaque on the wall. It's about achieving general overall principles.

"Our ultimate goal is to exceed our customers' expectations. To do that, we have to follow disciplines. Over the years, I have come to the conclusion that quality is vitally important, not just price. If we provide quality, customers will come to us with the next order."

UNIVERSITY HOSPITALS OF CLEVELAND

Location: Cleveland, Ohio.

President and CEO: Farah M. Walters.

People: 7,273 employees and physicians, including a medical staff comprised of 553 faculty and 624 residents.

History: Founded in 1866; named Lakeside Hospital in 1888. A formal affiliation agreement was signed in 1895 with Western Reserve University School of Medicine. Shortly after, a new hospital was built in University Circle, modeled after the innovative pavilion design of Johns Hopkins University Hospital.

                 Pediatric and obstetric services were established, and in the mid-1920s these joined with Lakeside Hospital to form University Hospitals of Cleveland (UHC). Over the years extensive patient care, teaching, and research facilities have been added.

Business: A 947-bed academic medical center, UHC serves Northeast Ohio and the nation through patient care, research, and teaching. UHC is the primary affiliate of Case Western Reserve University; together they form Ohio's largest biomedical research center.

                 In anticipation of and in response to changes in health-care delivery, UHC has evolved into University Hospitals Health System (UHHS), a regional health-care delivery system that includes a broad network of primary-care physicians, specialists, outpatient centers, and hospitals as well as related health-care delivery services.

Sales: For UHC, 42,362 discharges.
                 System-wide for UHHS, 51,054 discharges and 2,157,685 outpatient visits; net patient revenue of $617,125,000.

Commentary

It can be argued that in recent years no business in America has been subjected to so much scrutiny, pressure, and change as has the health-care industry.

The situation is compounded by the fact that to a great extent the customer is not one, but two: the one who receives care and the one who pays. The payer has pushed hospitals to move more services out of the hospital stay and to compress the remaining services into an ever-shorter length of stay.

And the product! While customer-payers demand a standardized product, insisting that a heart bypass is a heart bypass is a heart bypass, customer-patients expect care and services to be delivered in an individualized and caring way—known in the trade as high-touch. It's a business where each and every customer is a unique mix of physical, mental, emotional, social, and environmental factors; moreover, the work performed involves not a piece of steel or a part to rework, but a human life, where rework often is not possible.

Health care is a business where CEOs work with service providers (physicians) who only recently have begun to agree that standard protocols should be followed, where most of these key players (physicians) are independent of the operating structure, and where the customer (patient) is the product.

Nowhere is daily business more complex than in institutions like University Hospitals of Cleveland, where teaching and research are as much a part of the mission as is patient care. Continuous improvement in this environment is not only expected; it is actively sought. Full-time physicians spend hours in the laboratory on research projects, seeking answers that will be incorporated into patient care.

The institution must deliver increasingly sophisticated services while striving to control its costs as much as possible. The organization must also obtain the enthusiastic commitment of all its employees to provide a level of service commensurate with customer expectations.

To do this, University Hospitals has not only redesigned many long-standing practices but has also introduced new concepts, many from the world of business, to advance to a new plateau that combines standardized high-tech processes with fully individualized high-touch patient care and service.

—WINOC

"In the research laboratory we can give a rat a stroke, and we can cure the rat. The frustration of the past 20 years is that we cannot cure a human being who has a stroke. The difference boils down to time. The rat is here in the lab. The human isn't here, so we can't treat him." Warren Selman, M.D., is a neurological surgeon and director of UHC's Center for Stroke.

Selman is focused on his mission: to reverse the effects of stroke. He works against the long-standing conviction that a stroke always results in impairment or death.

"Time, time, time," worries Selman. A stroke can and must be treated in the first few hours, while the brain cells involved are injured but still alive; after that the window closes, the cells are dead, and action is useless. The difficulty is compounded by the fact that there are two types of strokes with two totally different causes and diametrically opposed therapies. So Selman made it his interim goal to buy time in those critical first hours by eliminating excess tests and tests done too late.

Eliminating excesses

While Selman wrestled with his dilemma, leadership wrestled with the need to become efficient. In the late 1980s, customer-payers weren't satisfied with just improvement in quality; they also wanted lower costs. All of UHC's sophistication of care, its teaching programs, and its clinical research—so integral to its mission—were the very things which drove up its costs beyond those of community and for-profit hospitals.

"We had to do things differently. We had to become effective *and* efficient. That meant we had to reach consensus on how we would provide care," says Charlene Phelps, R.N., Senior Vice President for Nursing. In 1989 Phelps and Michael Nochomovitz, M.D., headed a task force of physicians charged with initiating the development of care paths, protocols which would set a basic standard of care given for specific diagnoses.

The task force, comprised of physicians and a few nurses, faced a system in which every staff physician had a personal and inviolate way of treating a disease. To survive and to function successfully in the new health-care environment, UHC needed to develop uniform standards of care, to define what needed to be done and when to comply with the requisite length of stay for each diagnosis.

Today, this is standard operating procedure; in 1989 it was almost unheard of. The initial task force led to the decision to form smaller groups of experts in specific diagnoses or procedures. One of the first small groups dealt with the care of stroke patients.

Anticipating physicians to respond by saying things such as, "I'm not participating in cookbook medicine," and "Nobody should tell us how to practice," Phelps sought a way to get the task force's first meeting on a productive track.

"Clinicians—physicians and nurses—respond well to data. We asked our Cost Information Management System for the data from the previous year on almost 400 patients discharged with a diagnosis of stroke." Among the results: patients averaged 1.5 CT scans; half the patients were discharged on anti-coagulant drugs, and half weren't.

The physicians responded immediately to the data. "Why did so many patients have a second CT scan? Why were anti-coagulant drugs prescribed for 50% of the patients?" And so it began. After some six months of meetings, the group produced a care path for stroke patients.

"A care path covers the basics," says Phelps. "It is a care plan that identifies common or expected problems and the care components or interventions that serve patients well. Nothing in it says a physician cannot individualize care. To develop these care paths, physicians and nurses came to the table to review new knowledge, to debate issues of care, and to reach consensus about approaches to care for specific diagnoses or procedures. In 1989 almost the only place where that had happened formally was Tufts University and New England Medical Center.

"We discovered and corrected internal systems that inadvertently created barriers, such as cumbersome scheduling procedures. Within two years of introducing the stroke care path, we saw a significant reduction in mortality and morbidity.

"Physicians saw we were asking them to put more discipline into how UHC approaches care because so many people are involved in the process. When the physicians saw positive results, they took ownership of the process and results. They even made presentations to the community, to physicians, to EMS technicians, and to the public."

One piece, one success at a time

The team has been a flexible and evolving entity, as different professions and divisions bring their energies to bear on various pieces of treating the large and complex diagnosis known as stroke.

"We worked to perfect the care patients received after a stroke, to maximize their outcome," says Suzanne Clemente, R.N., head nurse of the Neuroscience Intensive Care Unit. "We developed a protocol for extended care because stroke has so many different causes and types that there's no single method of treatment. We worked with the agencies we discharged patients to, educating them about what happened to each patient and streamlining the care he or she will need.

"We started with one piece of stroke care, and as we got each piece working well, we added more pieces and brought more players to the table. It has been a long process; we did it in segments that were huge issues at the time we dealt with them. Each new piece brings key people and new momentum."

Measuring outcomes

In tracking outcomes, UHC monitors five areas in detail. The first, and always most important, is the clinical outcome. The second area is patient function at discharge. The third is health status, a combination of physical and emotional components from the patient's perspective. The fourth is patient satisfaction. The fifth area, although important, is always last: cost.

The added cost of innovations in care may be outweighed by long-term advantages. For example, in a pilot study of emergency treatment for one type of stroke, UHC physicians used an intra-arterial injection of the drug urokinase. There was an insignificant increase in cost, but a statistically significant improvement in results for 30-60% of patients, depending on the type of stroke. These patients returned home, perhaps to work, rather than to an institution, which produces long-term savings.

Brain attack, paradigm attack

Business management concepts and terms have filtered into the delivery of health care. Dr. Selman and his team are keen to bring about a significant paradigm shift. The prevailing and time-honored paradigm holds that nothing can be done for stroke beyond stabilizing patients and discharging them to another institution for rehabilitation or extended care. In this paradigm, physicians in all specialties say, "I can take care of a stroke. It's simple to manage. Why does it need a special medical team or nursing unit?" and even "I don't admit stroke patients to the hospital."

The term brain attack has been coined to combat this paradigm and to instill the sense of urgency and action historically associated with heart attacks.

"In the heart," says Selman, "if an area the size of a postage stamp fails, you can go on with your life if you get proper care. But if you lose the same volume of cells in your brain, and if that area controls a vital function such as speech, *and* if you don't get the right care fast, you lose the ability to understand others or to communicate with them. You as you know yourself will cease to exist. Isn't that an emergency?"

The ability to reverse strokes was greatly boosted in the early 1990s with the advent of revolutionary new technologies, including diagnostic MR imaging.

"People view new technology as expensive and impersonal," says Selman, "but it's the essence of specialized care. It leads to individualized care, to less pain and less risk." Unlike national research, which provides a sweeping overview and a guide, UHC's new technology aims to provide selectivity and can look at individual patients' needs.

Selman formed a three-member stroke team with Robert Tarr, M.D., the Director of Interventional Neuroradiology, and Dennis Landis, M.D., the Director of Neurology. They came in at all hours, whenever a stroke patient arrived in Emergency. The team knew it would take *one* success to convince others. They were lucky. A 70-year-old man had a massive stroke and was luckily brought to Emergency. The brain attack team did its job, and the patient, instead of dying, went home.

It's still an uphill struggle for the team. Despite talking to community physicians, EMS teams, and the public at every opportunity, the team finds the old paradigm still entrenched. The job is not yet done.

The big picture

"Care paths are just one tool involved in developing an environment and workforce where people at all levels in the organization embrace change and constantly seek to improve quality and service responsiveness," says Farah Walters, CEO.

"It sounds like a cliche, but it's true: in our set of values, the needs of the patient and family must always come first as the primary focus of our attention, and so we treat them like our own family—and we are always willing to ask how to do things better, and unafraid to acknowledge when we're wrong. When there's a problem, if the service was less than it should be, we fix it.

"Most barriers in business are created internally, not externally. If we create barriers to better service because of internal structures, there's nowhere to go but downward. If we lose in the health-care market, it's a result not of competition, but of steps we didn't take, of patient needs we ignored, of problems we didn't solve."

In 1992 Walters took a very big step. "I put my career on the line. I directed a total shift in strategy that moved away from a horizontal, loose affiliation of hospitals to a vertical, fully integrated health-care delivery system. This was a radical departure from what was considered correct by all the other elite academic medical centers in the U.S. Everybody in those centers was convinced they would always have enough patients no matter what happened in the health-care environment, and that the payers of health care would continue to pay for the charges associated with educating the next generation of physicians. When managed care hit the market, academic centers became vulnerable.

"We had to think very differently in a proactive way. Before, our chief focus had always been those patients who need the most advanced care. Now we had to convince academicians that maybe we don't need more MRIs or another ICU, but that we do need to provide primary care and prevention in, for example, Westlake and Twinsburg and Geauga County. That required enormous changes on the part of physicians, trustees, and employees. We started designing and building a total high-quality system, from the outside in."

UHC expanded into University Hospitals Health System (UHHS), a regional health-care delivery system that includes a broad network of primary-care physicians, specialists, outpatient centers, and hospitals; wellness programs, occupational health, skilled nursing, elder health, home care, and rehabilitation; and QualChoice Health Plan, managed care and insurance.

The employee's role in the total system

In the process of developing this system, it was important to give all UHC employees an understanding of the changes in the health-care environment and what that means to them as employees, how UHC will carry out its mission in this changing environment, and the impact of employees' behaviors on UHC's success. This was done through Foundations, an educational program that is part of the User-Friendly Initiative introduced in 1995.

"We provided a comprehensive conceptualization of who we are and who we are becoming, and why," says Phelps. "We need to retain what we do well and improve what we need to improve, and employees need to be an integral part of the process. They need to understand why we ask them to reduce costs at the same time that we invest in other areas of our business.

"It's important not only to spend on bricks and mortar and on high-tech equipment—$500 million in the past decade—but also to put forth money, time, and effort on developing people and their skills in redesigning systems and in working with people."

"This program has shown employees how important their role is to the success of the organization," says Mary Lou Anderson, Director of Physician and Guest Relations. She co-chairs the Foundations taskforce, which has 55 members drawn from many departments and levels in the organization.

"The Foundations program has helped employees make better sense of what they see at work as well as in the community and in the media. They had heard bits and pieces; now they know how everything fits together—the environment and what UH is doing to respond.

"As one- and two-day hospital stays become common, this knowledge becomes more crucial. There's very little time to get to know patients, and employees must communicate and work effectively with their peers to negotiate such a big system so fast—and without losing the caring quality and compassion."

UHC has a history of employee caring in a high-tech setting. That tradition has been confirmed by surveys conducted by Cleveland Health Quality Choice, an independent nonprofit organization that rates medical care and patient satisfaction for hospitals throughout a four-county area. In 1995 and 1996, UHC received the highest ratings among all hospitals for global patient satisfaction from medical-surgical patients.

"That attitude has to be fostered, developed, and renewed," says Anderson. "Our goal is 'Exceptional service every time.' Our standards of service are basic: smile and be friendly; focus on the patient; respect others; be courteous; respond quickly and explain delays; be helpful; look the part. Each employee has control over doing these things and excelling at them. If we all did them all the time, what a difference it would make!"

Quality throughout the continuum of care

"UHC is part of a continuum of care," says Walters. "It's a strong university hospital giving access to the most advanced medicine, science, and technology. It's not the hub of the system: that would mean every one of the people served by UHHS will be cared for here. UHHS has a goal of enrolling 750,000 *people* in it, most of them healthy. Many of the people enrolled in UHHS never will come here or should. But they do have access to primary care at the same level of quality."

VAN DORN DEMAG CORPORATION

Location: Strongsville, Ohio (headquarters).
              Brunswick and Cleveland, Ohio; Fountain Inn and
              Duncan, South Carolina.

President and CEO: William G. (Jerry) Pryor.

People: 800.

History: Founded in 1872 as the Van Dorn Company, which
              manufactured iron products and accessories; product
              introductions included the hand-held drill and the now-
              ubiquitous flip-top can.

              In the 1940s Van Dorn was one of the first U.S. companies
              to produce injection-molding machines. In 1946 the
              company took part in the first National Plastics Exhibition.

              Van Dorn was acquired in 1993 by Crown Cork & Seal
              Company. It kept two divisions, both container
              companies. The third division, Van Dorn Plastic
              Machinery Company, was sold to Mannesmann Demag
              AG (Germany) and was merged with Mannesmann's
              already-existing U.S. operation to form Van Dorn Demag.

              Mannesmann AG is the world's largest manufacturer
              in the industry, with six injection-molding
              manufacturers in the U.S. and Europe. The merger gave
              Van Dorn Demag a distribution network that facilitated
              access to international markets.

Business: Manufacturer of injection-molding machines for
              automotive, appliance, housewares, electronics,
              medical, and other industries.

              Annually produces 1,000-1,200 machines, many of them
              custom-designed. Machines have clamping force, or
              tonnage capacity, of 85 to 4,400 tons.

Sales: $250 million.

Commentary

From being a textbook example of old cultures and systems that no longer worked in the new business environment, Van Dorn Demag made steady progress into Total Quality Management (TQM) that encompasses all areas of the business. The company also has become a benchmark for other Northeast Ohio companies that have tackled TQM.

The creation of Van Dorn Demag's quality system began with the hiring of Dave Udovich. Charged with the responsibility of "getting a quality system," he tackled his assignment with absolute zeal, by direct and indirect routes.

The TQM process received a real boost with the advent of CEO Jerry Pryor, who knew how beneficial TQM could be. The company's acquisition by an international conglomerate could easily have derailed TQM efforts, but that obviously did not happen here—the German parent company is interested in the cost-effective TQM strategies Van Dorn has implemented.

The rest, as they say, is history: a transformed company capable of reclaiming the lead in its industry.

—WINOC

There was no joy at Van Dorn in the mid-1980s. After decades as king of the hill, this manufacturer of injection-molding machinery was catapulted into survival strategy mode. Otherwise Van Dorn would face its final inning and the industry would migrate overseas, just as VCRs, cameras, and robots had done.

Van Dorn's machines were built to endure and were installed in more U.S. factories than the machines of any competitor. Now the company suddenly found its market share being eroded by newcomers: lower-priced Japanese machines that were slower but very reliable and that established a new definition of quality in the marketplace.

Van Dorn not only lost the market lead but also began experiencing customer dissatisfaction, expressed in warranty losses. In addition, the company was unequipped to deal with new technology, especially microprocessors and proportional hydraulics.

Starting the turnaround

In early 1986, Van Dorn hired Dave Udovich as Director of Quality. A former design engineer, he describes himself as "a long-time zealot in quality." He had attended a Toronto quality conference before quality was talked about, had met Deming, and had worked at Westinghouse, where he helped write that company's original quality manual.

"In 1986 Van Dorn's quality was not good, as measured by customer complaints, warranty losses, and cost of waste. Our first task was to stop the heavy bleeding caused by warranty problems and to get a handle on the new technologies."

He began preliminary quality planning by assembling an Ishikawa diagram, delineating cause and effect of warranty and other problems resulting from manufactured components, purchased parts, assembly, and test nonconformance. He quickly discovered that Van Dorn had no clear-cut definition of quality, and no ownership or accountability for quality problems. Also, the company heavily emphasized the detection of defects in finished product, with very little emphasis on prevention.

"We built the product and then exhaustively inspected it to make sure it ran. We were inspecting for quality rather than building it in.

"The existing systems and culture were also part of the problem. The company was very autocratic. Employees were expected to park their brains outside the door and follow orders. When Japan and Europe took the lead, Van Dorn became a follower, and we didn't have the infrastructure to follow fast enough, nor were we tapping our most important resource—our people's abilities and creativity."

Piece by piece, page by page, a detailed quality plan evolved. But plans, being proactive by nature, were out of sync with the reactionary management environment. So Udovich shared the details with his quality staff and advised his boss on a need-to-know basis. "If there had been a company plan, it would have been implemented by brute force. We didn't have leadership at that time—we had management by fear."

By 1988 change had begun, but incrementally, emanating up, down, and laterally from the Quality Department. "My boss had been very successful at taking the division from inception to $120 million. At that point a business can no longer be run solely from on high. Trust and decision-making must be cascaded so the organization can continue to grow."

The external environment finally drove the company to begin implementing TQM in earnest. Market share had begun to decline in the early 1980s, with over 50% of U.S. demand filled by offshore producers, and profits had begun to decline in 1987. Domestic manufacturers had dropped from 20 to 4. And the market had intensified its demands in terms of quality, lead time, price, and technology.

Udovich was grasping for a way to do what he'd been hired to do. He returned from a seminar on how to make the transition from traditional to participative management and how to empower employee teams to function entrepreneurially. He told his boss, "I sat next to my counterpart at X—, and they're going to do all this."

X— was Van Dorn's chief competitor. Whatever X— did, Van Dorn immediately followed suit. And so TQM really began at Van Dorn. The company sent three of its top managers—the heads of manufacturing, information technology, and quality—to be trained as trainers in participative management, empowerment, and coaching. The three returned and trained all supervisory staff, down to and including team leaders.

On the basis of that understanding, the next step was taken: to develop employees' ability to solve problems, and to take ownership for their jobs and processes and for the company's success. Employees were empowered to form problem-solving teams (called QAT, or Quality Action Teams) to pursue continuous improvement. These processes have become so much a part of Van Dorn culture that they are self-perpetuating.

Full steam ahead

A great many processes were introduced in quick succession: formulation of quality values; training in participative management; introduction of cost of quality; and Quality Function Deployment (QFD), a structured system which captures the voice of the customer and uses customer wants and needs to drive new-product development and continuous improvement throughout the organization. Automated testing of subassemblies also began very early to achieve quality at the source and to support Just-In-Time manufacturing principles to build quality into everything the company does.

Supplier management was introduced. Because suppliers contribute 60% of the cost of equipment manufactured by Van Dorn Demag, management of the supplier process offered significant opportunities and was essential to the company's continuous improvement objectives. The division's head of purchasing was eager to work on this piece, which provided one of Van Dorn's early wins in TQM.

The key was to escape the adversarial approach and replace it with long-term win-win partnerships, built on a mutual commitment to TQM principles. The result: significantly fewer suppliers and substantially improved supplier quality, competitiveness, and delivery.

Next came a formal suggestion process for improving quality (Corrective Action System), skills development and training, and awareness and recognition of employees.

New impetus at the top

With the arrival of Jerry Pryor at Van Dorn in 1989 as corporate Senior Vice President, TQM finally received the top-management level of support it needed in order to take hold. "The group here had investigated TQM and was at an early stage of commitment," says Pryor. "Van Dorn had started on individual components of quality, and at that time concepts such as quality circles and JIT had not yet been assimilated into TQM.

"When TQM is new to a company, the gains aren't apparent to its leaders and they find it hard to justify the approach. Coming from one of the first U.S. companies to adopt Japanese management concepts, I knew first-hand that TQM could produce benefits."

With the sale of the division to Mannesmann Demag in 1993, Pryor became President and CEO. His charge: to improve competitiveness and profitability and to regain market share position. "We are the second largest manufacturer of injection-molding machinery in the U.S., and as part of Mannesmann AG we are part of the world's largest manufacturer."

In 1989 Van Dorn had created a vision: to be the best world-class manufacturer of plastic processing machinery. In 1991, for the first time, a summary of the strategic plan was shared with all employees. Before then, nothing about the business had been shared with employees; sales figures were given only when it was necessary to push people harder or when times were tough and layoffs were imminent.

That vision was translated into the five internal components by which it would be achieved:
1. Just In Time acknowledges time as a strategically important issue.
2. Total Preventive Maintenance stresses the need to do things right the first time, to make the transition from detection to prevention. By 1996, for example, TQM enabled Van Dorn Demag to reduce its

inspectors from 28 to 5, and the mission is to eliminate formal inspection entirely, possibly by the year 2000, now that Van Dorn is attuned to quality at the source and to statistical process control.

3. Associate Involvement and Empowerment is essential to unleash the creativity of the company's most important asset, its people.
4. Design For Manufacturability asks, "Do we have the people, product technology, and equipment capable of doing it, and if not, is it so important that we must adapt in order to be able to do it?"
5. Total Quality Assurance asks, "Do we have a quality system and the discipline necessary to achieve consistent quality and reliability to assure customer satisfaction?" That is, do we have the mindset for continuous improvement, prevention, quality at the source, management by fact, supplier development, and quality as a way of life?

One of the first pieces developed in the TQM process was a survey to determine customer satisfaction. Van Dorn Demag now sends a survey 6-8 weeks after a machine is installed, does a follow-up 18 months later, and has begun further follow-ups by an independent company. With a commitment to continuous improvement, Van Dorn Demag expects survey results to improve steadily.

The elements of TQM

The company's TQM model shows 14 elements of TQM. It's no coincidence that the model echoes Deming's teachings and the criteria used by the Malcolm Baldridge National Quality Award. "I stole shamelessly," says Udovich, "from benchmarking studies, seminars, and professionals."

All 14 elements of Van Dorn's TQM model were initially implemented by the Quality Department. Some were eventually taken over by other departments. For example, Quality Action Teams and Quality Awareness and Recognition were deployed to Human Resources, which monitors and sanctions teams and coordinates all aspects of recognition; cost-of-quality measure was deployed to Finance; Quality Function Deployment, to Marketing; supplier management, to Purchasing; and automated testing, to Manufacturing.

Quality Function Deployment is the means by which Van Dorn Demag introduced a culture and an infrastructure for innovation. Innovation is sought in services as well as in products, and innovation in services often provides a competitive advantage.

Cross-functional teams obtain an understanding of customer wants and needs, and new products are developed accordingly. Today Van Dorn Demag again has two sides to its business: development of new products and services, and fulfillment of orders for current products and services.

The purchase of new injection molding machines requires a customer company to make a sizable investment in teaching employees about its operation and maintenance, so a molder needs overwhelming reasons to switch to a new type of equipment provided by a new supplier.

Insulating customers from change

"It's our job to insulate our customers from the impact of change," says Udovich. "We must make it clear that with our product they will realize maximum value, immediately and long-term, and that they can run the new machine with the absolute minimum investment in training."

Injection-molding machines are put in computer-hostile environments with heat, humidity, dirt, shock, vibration, and pollution. Besides being unable to tolerate these conditions, commercially available computer control systems lacked many features that are needed and included some unnecessary ones.

Quality Function Deployment, Design For Manufacturability, and other TQM initiatives enabled Van Dorn Demag to achieve particular success when it decided to design its own control systems for its machines.

"Customers told us the control system had to be user-friendly. That term is very popular and usually vague. Our prototype machine control design was driven by customer wants and needs which defined user-friendly in real terms. We interviewed some 20 customers—hundreds of individuals—to determine and rank specific wants.

"We brought in customers to test it; we also brought in a class of 9th-graders to see if we could teach it to them. In addition, the hardware and software went through extensive alpha and beta site testing before introduction to identify and remove bugs."

Software posed another challenge. In the past, company engineers designed a program, then took it out into the plant to test it on the actual machine. There were complaints from external and internal customers about software defects.

A process-improvement team was commissioned with the charge: "How can we improve the quality of our software?" For its benchmarks, the team researched or visited Carnegie Mellon, Allen Bradley, and IBM Houston (creator of software for NASA's space shuttle).

After a cross-functional team has performed a QFD, the team designs the machine's computer control accordingly. A control's success is evaluated in terms of a number of measurements: customer acceptance, achievement of cost targets, what percent of the customer's target performance attributes have been met, growth in market share, and profitability.

As a result, Van Dorn Demag has developed software to recognized state-of-the-art programming standards, has bought programming computers for each of its software engineers, and has designed and constructed simulators to assure quality at the source. Today the company has virtually eliminated software defects, resulting in customer satisfaction.

The shining star of the Quality Function Deployment (QFD) process is the Pathfinder series of controls, a family of control systems designed and built specifically for the injection-molding industry. Pathfinder was judged Best of Show at the national plastics exhibition in Chicago in 1994. Just one year later, almost 100% of Van Dorn Demag's customers had switched from the control they previously ordered to the Pathfinder control.

This switch is unprecedented, and the QFD process has indeed become a way of life. Van Dorn Demag attributes a number of successful new products to QFD, which will drive the design of all its future products. Today the company again seeks patents on its new designs and is selectively taking the lead, introducing innovative technologies in its products.

Customer Application Team: the new wheel

Formerly, Sales handed off a customer order to Engineering, which tried to interpret, with little guidance from Sales, what the customer wanted and how to configure the machine. As a result, machines didn't quite meet customer expectations and options subsequently had to be added, making the entire process lengthy, cumbersome, and sometimes late.

Van Dorn formed a team in 1990 to improve the order process and chartered the Customer Application Team in 1992. Van Dorn Demag now focuses on prevention-based continuous improvement, on both process and product.

Sales, manufacturing, and engineering functions come together as the Customer Application Team; offices are situated in spokes off a central hub, where these functions as a team tackle new orders for machines with special configurations.

The result is a product closely configured to the customer's needs. And with the emphasis shifted from inspection to prevention, machines are also produced and tested much more quickly: the quote-to-ship process, which previously took 12-25 weeks, now averages 3-12 weeks.

The whole company is working toward common objectives; and JIT has been integrated throughout every function of the organization. The key JIT elements adopted are focused-factory concepts, Kanban material principles, and throughput reduction. Within two years of beginning JIT, Van Dorn Demag doubled its overseas sales.

ISO, CE, and Baldridge

The push for ISO 9000 certification was a natural progression. ISO supported Van Dorn's continuous improvement efforts by solidifying discipline in the quality system to enable management-by-fact, thereby bringing integrity to prevention efforts. Quality planning was already being done; ISO required that its documentation be stepped up. Van Dorn Demag achieved ISO certification in March, 1994, after just 9 months of preparation.

"ISO has been a great motivator," says Pryor. "Everybody is proud we did it so quickly, and we got many compliments from outsiders, who were astonished we did so much so fast."

In January, 1996, the company faced the need to obtain CE product certification in order to qualify for free distribution of its machines to Europe. Typically taking a company 3-4 years, this certification was achieved by Van Dorn Demag in less than 4 months, another yeoman's task which was achieved more quickly thanks to TQM.

Going beyond ISO, Van Dorn Demag has begun to use as one of its benchmarks the Malcolm Baldridge standard, which has strong parallels to Van Dorn Demag's core business values. The similarity is no coincidence: for several years Udovich has been on the Malcolm Baldridge Board of Examiners, and Van Dorn Demag plans to apply for the Baldridge award.

Challenges for the future

"The challenge," says Pryor, "is to stay committed to quality and to continuous improvement. As the new vision and quality concepts become a way of life for us, the new plateau of performance is quickly accepted as the new standard. It's difficult to continue to make big strides, so it's hard to keep the commitment going. The challenge is to answer the question, 'How do we improve next?'

"I see one advantage for Van Dorn Demag in this respect. We have learned from others. For example, WINOC helped early on by making a Baldridge assessment to evaluate the TQM processes, doing a gap analysis to help formulate strategic planning issues, and making a pre-assessment of compliance to ISO standards before ISO was a hot topic.

"We are to a great extent self-educated in TQM. As a result, people throughout the organization have taken far more ownership in the process.

"We have made tremendous strides with TQM. We aren't excellent in all areas, but we aren't low in any either. Very few companies can dedicate sufficient resources in all areas and be fiscally responsible. That's why we are on a never-ending journey of continuous improvement. We pick what's important to our customers. Because we cannot afford or devote unlimited resources, we focus on what we can do best. There's always more to do."

Being in a very competitive industry, Van Dorn Demag must stay very aggressive and focused on the customer and the TQM process.

"TQM requires people to wear several hats," says Udovich. "There is TQM, the work at hand, and the crisis of the day. There are constant new motivations to keep committed to quality improvements, and every improvement, major and minor, involves change."

Measures of performance and success

In a formal quarterly review process Van Dorn Demag uses over 40 metrics to measure its performance in three areas: cost, quality, and market share. All three areas are considered equally important and closely interrelated. The company identifies three key contributors to success in total quality:

1. Continued focus on understanding the customer's changing needs and using that information to redesign, make, and service the product to meet or exceed customer expectations;

2. Commitment to product quality via redesign and quality processes; and discipline of consistent manufacture to ISO 9001 quality system requirements; and
3. Application of JIT throughout the organization, recognizing the strategic importance of time, focused factories, quality at the source, Kanban material control, and aggressive throughput reduction.

Between 1992 and 1995, Van Dorn Demag's market share increased by more than 30% (it grew again in 1996), in a time when other domestic and foreign producers lost market share or held level. In that same period, pretax income, as measured by machine shipments, more than doubled as a percent of sales; and sales per employee more than doubled to over $250,000.

TQM has enabled Van Dorn to get to a very different place. The company is cost-effective. It produces a reliable product and has recaptured market share. It has evolved into a culture of participative management. It now taps the creative resources of its people and enables them to be proactive problem-solvers. It now thrives on new technology. But most of all, Van Dorn Demag recognizes it is in business for and because of its customers.

Zircoa, Inc.

Location: Solon, Ohio.

President: John A. Kaniuk.

People: 150.

History: Founded in 1952; business ownership changed several times in the early years. In 1988 Zircoa became a wholly owned subsidiary of Didier-Werke AG, Wiesbaden, Germany.

In the early years Zircoa worked with NASA's Lewis Research Center on yttrium-stabilized zirconia plasma spray powders. This work led to adoption of the thermal-barrier coating that is now the standard on modern aircraft engines and other similar applications.

Business: Manufacturer of industrial products made of zirconia powder for applications that require resistance to extreme heat, extreme corrosion, or contamination. Products include specialty powders, refractories, and ceramics.

Sales: $18 million.

Commentary

Among Zircoa's many strengths, two areas are particularly noteworthy: extensive employee training and a gain sharing system that gives employees outstanding opportunities for involvement and for sharing in Zircoa's success.

Many gain sharing plans fail because too much time is spent looking for the perfect formula. It doesn't exist. If it did, development of the plan would be simple. Zircoa created a formula that has proven to be a very successful one. It was created by the employees who participate in the plan.

Equally if not more important, Zircoa's people linked the gain sharing plan to the company's long-range plan for continuous improvement: the plan is linked to employee involvement, improvement of work processes, and customer satisfaction.

Employees have the opportunity to create gains, and they understand the plan's most heavily weighted factors, which Zircoa calls speeds and selects. No system is perfect, but, all things considered, Zircoa's comes as close as any we know of.

If developed and implemented correctly, gain sharing creates a sense of ownership in the continued viability of an organization. It gives everyone an opportunity to participate in the creation of tangible gains—and to share equally in those gains.

A major factor in Zircoa's success is training. Zircoa trained all employees extensively in communications, problem-solving, and teamwork—and gives them ongoing opportunities to use those skills. In 1992, the year after the gain sharing plan was developed, Zircoa spent 6% of employee time in training. Ongoing employee training averages 2.5% per year, probably putting Zircoa near the 90th percentile of U.S. firms their size in commitment to training.

This training was a demonstration of the commitment to employee involvement and continuous improvement. And it was a demonstration that the commitment was more than just talk. It was a commitment to provide to all employees the skills that enable them to succeed in their efforts to improve upon those performance measures that are in their control. This is what has made gain sharing a success at Zircoa. People make the difference.

—WINOC

The plant manager made a list of the nine people he wanted to see on Zircoa's Gain Sharing Committee. A similar list was made by the president of the union, American Flint Glass Workers Local #1033.

The plant manager and the union president had agreed on four rules for making their lists. One, select six hourly people and three salaried people. Two, exclude union officials and company managers. Three, include some experienced people with a knowledge of different parts of the plant and some new people without preconceived ideas. Four, include a former union leader and an accounting person.

Then the union president and the plant manager swapped lists and got down to the business of agreeing on a single list: Zircoa's Gain Sharing Committee.

That was the easy part. "We got quick agreement on the people," says John Kaniuk, Zircoa's President. "For the next two months they received a lot of training. They learned how to function effectively as a team, and they learned a lot about gain sharing—what it is, the different types of programs, and how they work."

The next step was the stumper. Working with a gain sharing consultant, the committee had to devise a formula for distribution of gains. The committee had been given full control and responsibility for the design of the plan. They ultimately would have to sell the plan, first to management, and then to all employees, union and nonunion.

It took the committee a year to do it. The top leaders waited, convinced that gain sharing was absolutely central to continuous improvement at Zircoa.

A philosophy of managing people

To understand why, one has to go back to the years when Kaniuk was growing up. His father was a miner and a union man, but he also wound up owner of a construction business and a grocery. He struggled to reconcile these opposite poles. He did it by consensus.

When the younger Kaniuk went to work as a supervisor in his dad's construction company, he too faced a dilemma.

"I knew nothing about construction, and I was the lowest paid, but I was in charge of people. I had to get consensus—otherwise nobody would have worked for me. Looking back, I see that I have always been thrown into things and have had to figure them out, and I have always tried to do it by consensus. I believe in it."

When he says consensus, he means exactly that: the time-intensive process in which people examine underlying interests, needs, and values in order to find the alternative everyone can agree to—to say, "For myself, I might not do it exactly this way, but I can live with this decision and support it as a member of this group."

"That's actually what my dad did, and that's what we do at Zircoa," says Kaniuk. "We need everyone to support and go in the same direction. Most corporations don't arrive at consensus, and then people go off and do their own thing."

Kaniuk arrived at Zircoa in 1990 and took charge in 1991. At the time Zircoa wasn't doing very well, and Kaniuk had to increase profitability. "You look at problems and decide what is going to be your business mode," he says. "Many companies choose the short-term solution and cut some positions. We changed our whole culture so we could solve problems and make the business profitable. Our management team decided a radical change was needed in philosophy, culture, and thinking."

The old management style had been very top-down. "Problems were viewed as engineering problems, and instead of training the people who perform the work to solve the problems, management hired ceramic engineers. So of course the hourly people said, 'Gee, I've got all these problems. You have to get out here and fix them.' People don't say that any more. If they did, we'd say, 'Fix it yourself!' "

Kaniuk had two basic (he calls them very simple) beliefs: "One, be honest with everybody; that includes respect for them and the contribution they can make. And two, put everybody in the same boat."

With that philosophy, Kaniuk, the plant manager, and the chief financial officer went looking for structure, for organizations to benchmark and for experts to advise. "From what I saw of other companies, they never put everyone in one boat. At that time TQM hadn't yet become a buzzword. We had bits and pieces from everywhere, but not a blueprint to follow."

The plan they finally adopted was based on the Malcolm Baldridge criteria. A key element of the plan is the empowerment of all employees to act independently or in groups to improve Zircoa's products and processes. A centerpiece of the plan is a gain sharing program that makes the company's goals the employees' goals and that builds trust among all parties so that people are unafraid to take action. In keeping with a consensus approach, the plan was communicated to all employees because it was critical for a majority of employees to understand and agree with the direction being taken.

Developing the gain sharing plan

Kaniuk believes that "putting everyone in one boat" is synonymous with gain sharing. So here we are again, waiting for the committee to devise its formula.

Why was this so hard for the committee to do? After all, they had a consultant helping them who had done hundreds of such plans. The committee concluded that every plan they looked at was too simple and didn't suit Zircoa's situation.

"Those plans were for production shops that made one thing. Or the plans didn't allow for differences in how each individual could have an impact on the numbers."

The first difficulty for Zircoa's Gain Sharing Committee was how to devise a system in which each individual could identify his or her own contribution. The second difficulty was how to devise a direct correlation between the job each individual does and the gain.

The complexity of the plan ultimately adopted reflects the complexity and diversity of Zircoa's products. Virtually every product is to a large extent custom-manufactured, and the manufacturing process is constantly changing. Ten lines are in operation at a time, some of them involving very different processes, and that's high for such a small company—125 people on the floor and 25 in support functions.

One substance Zircoa works with, zirconium oxide, is a unique crystalline compound with remarkable qualities: very little erosion, contamination-free, and a very good insulator at very high temperatures; the manufacturing process developed with NASA involves temperatures at 5,000°F.

Through a variety of chemical compositions and a variety of manufacturing processes, zirconia can be tailored to meet very different and demanding needs.

For example, zirconia nozzles can survive unscathed after hundreds of tons of molten steel have poured through at temperatures as high as 3,200°F. Crucibles for the aerospace industry must withstand thermal shock and resist erosion. Spray powders are used to coat machinery that needs thermal barriers or surfaces that resist corrosion or erosion. On any given day Zircoa can be manufacturing all these products and more.

The committee finally came up with a formula that took three major factors into account in determining each individual's share: first, the productivity with which a job is performed (speed); second, the amount of prime product generated (selects); and three, the dollars required by the first two factors (spending).

Zircoa's workforce has a very broad range of skills. There are people who run batching operations or pressing equipment where ceramics are formed under pressure; people who supervise a shift; people who are machinists by trade; people who are shift leaders, managing a continuous process and the people who do it; and people who are skilled operators of high-temperature furnaces and who use the latest programmable electronics.

In December 1991, the committee presented its formula. Selling the plan was not easy because of its complexity; in fact, the committee's consultant recommended against the plan for that very reason. The committee, however, believed in the plan and overwhelmingly sold it to the employees: it won 87% approval.

All savings are calculated according to the formula; half goes to the company, and the other half is divided equally among all employees.

"We started the program in 1991, before it was completed," says Kaniuk. "We told our people we would use mid-1990 as our baseline and would calculate gains once the program was established. In this way we hoped everybody could be working on improvements. Our numbers started to take off in January, 1992, only after the program was understood and accepted."

As Kaniuk sees it, gain sharing topped off his work to establish trust, which he calls his number-one job. Communication is also essential to building trust. Zircoa has monthly meetings for all employees as well as small-group meetings. Kaniuk tells employees where Zircoa stands and what it needs. "I tell the truth and answer questions. When the head of the company shares *all* the numbers with employees and fields all the questions about those numbers, a lot of the mistrust goes away."

Zircoa also has profit sharing: 4% of salaries is put into a pool, and the payout can range from 0 to 8%, depending on company profits. Participants can lose their 4% if Zircoa falls short of their agreed-upon profit goals; conversely, if profits are high, employees get 8%. To date the union has chosen not to put any wages at risk, although it always has the opportunity to participate, so only salaried employees participate in profit sharing at this time.

Training people to make the system succeed

With the gain sharing plan in place, the Gain Sharing Committee became Zircoa's Steering Committee, working with people on the shop floor, helping them understand what they could do to affect the gain, answering their questions about details of the gain sharing plan, helping facilitate groups that tackled improvements in quality and productivity throughout the company, and determining what training was needed.

The committee convinced management that all employees needed to improve their skills in communications and in problem-solving in order for Zircoa (and gain sharing) to succeed. Each employee received three full days of training off-site by WINOC in the skills necessary to communicate and resolve conflicts and problems without resorting to an arbitrator or supervisor. This training was key to Zircoa's ability to solve problems and create improvements.

After this training, communication improved between management and employees. Monthly hour-long meetings were held with all employees for communication and open discussion. These meetings resulted in mutual agreement that employees needed more basic skill training in order to keep Zircoa moving forward. This training would allow employees to better understand all the new information on job performance as well as documenting how the jobs would be performed.

Extensive commitment to training and education

A grant funded by the U.S. Department of Education provided all employees with training in communications and in job-related mathematics. A confidential assessment of basic skills indicated some deficits in math skills but high communications skills. An advanced communications course was designed that addressed how to deal with difficult people, and how to listen and to express oneself effectively. All employees have taken this course at full company expense.

Next came specific training—machine setup, blueprint reading, computer use. This training occurs on a continuing basis and is conducted mostly off-the-job to assure that employees understand practical applications and benefits. There is also refresher training in problem-solving skills. And every new hire attends WINOC's facilitator workshop, which teaches not only how teams function but also gives team members an understanding of the facilitator role in the success of a team.

The basic skills training was important to employees for several reasons. It showed people they were still capable of learning and, because much of the training was done via computer, that they didn't have to be afraid of technology. It also showed the difference between intelligence and knowledge, so that employees were unafraid to seek help.

With 140 computers at Zircoa, computer training is essential. People use the computer daily: to report their work on a real-time basis, to get a print of a part (hard-copy blueprints are unavailable), to record their time for payroll purposes, and to keep meeting notes. Training is done on company time, and employees are responsible for scheduling their work so that production is met. Orders are completed on time, and productivity is better than it ever has been.

In 1992 Zircoa spent over 6% of employee time in training. Since then, it has averaged 2.5%. In addition, a learning lab was set up, equipped with computers and self-paced programs. Here employees can spend one hour each week on company time to learn on their own, with an instructor available at certain times. Over a five-year period, Zircoa's training program has included the following components, many of them on an ongoing basis:

- group facilitator training (four days for every employee);
- experienced facilitator training as needed;
- basic skills in math and communications;
- set-up reduction, specific to the department and equipment;
- skilled trades apprenticeship (state-accredited) in machine shop and maintenance, for current and prospective employees;
- blueprint reading (geometric tolerancing 1&2) as needed, and for all second-shift employees;
- basic electronics, as needed;
- educational assistance, including completion of degree, for employees at all levels;
- computer training in a number of software programs;
- job-specific training, such as technology updates and time management;
- CAD-CAM, in the few instances where applicable;
- refresher of basic skills;
- safety-related issues;
- first aid;
- statistical process control; and
- effective listening.

Training has been embraced by employees and management as being essential to Zircoa's growth and stability. Training is a primary tool for progress and for closely interwoven benefits, as it leads to job satisfaction, monetary rewards, and job security.

Numbers tell of dramatic improvement

While Zircoa hasn't formally measured job satisfaction per se, there are indicators of dramatic improvements. Absenteeism is down from 2% to 1.3%. Turnover remains at almost zero. Grievances dropped from 35 to 5 per year.

Financial success came quickly once gain sharing was implemented. Operating expenses dropped by $700,000 in the first year; of that total, 95% was due to employee efforts to improve product and process quality. The result of these savings was a turnaround from an operating loss in 1991 to a respectable operating profit of 10% of sales in 1992. Quality savings under the gain sharing program resulted in each employee receiving about $900 in gain sharing distribution for the first year, 1992. Each employee received more than $2,000 in 1995.

Job security has also improved dramatically. Monthly layoffs and callbacks had been routine for union employees. Since 1993 there have been no layoffs.

"Zircoa's results have exceeded all the goals we originally anticipated," says Kaniuk. "A major surprise was that employees set very high goals which require continued improvement and training. We have been very active in promoting our philosophy and accomplishments to our parent company, to our customers, and to our suppliers. We believe it is one of our strengths, and we use it as a sales tool so that others will want to partner with us. We also take every opportunity to have our customers meet our employees. We always get the order when a customer sees the commitment of our employees.

"Also, in most companies, the thrust of the gain sharing program is to do the job at lower cost; Zircoa's program is based on what the customer really wants. We develop a really good product and are able to charge a fair price for it." In 1996 fully 20% of Zircoa's product line consists of new products. "The first time you ask the customer what they want and solve their problem, you get their trust. When the customer sees the results, they tell you they have another problem because they want you to work with them to solve that, too."

For publishing information, see Bibliography (page 209).

Assessment

Every organization should have 1996 Award Criteria: Malcolm Baldridge National Quality Award on its bookshelf. The National Institute of Standards and Technology (NIST) updates this resource annually.

A good basic article is D. Garvin's "How the Baldridge Award Really Works." A useful book on the subject is Mark Graham Brown's Baldridge Award Winning Quality: How to Interpret the Malcolm Baldridge Award Criteria.

The 1973 Annual Handbook for Group Facilitators, edited by Jones and Pfeiffer, gives in-depth information on how to use the concept of the Johari Window, which was developed by Joseph Luft and Harry Ingham.

Leadership

Three successful leaders with very different styles give their approach and philosophy in these three videos. In Flight of the Buffalo, James Belasco draws on considerable real-life experience and insight as he addresses how to effect the transformation from the buffalo style of leadership, where one leader is to be followed blindly and permanently, to an airborne style that supports high performance. In If Enough People Care, Lou Holtz, Notre Dame coach, gives an inspiring and entertaining pep talk on his philosophy of coaching his football team. In Speed, Simplicity, and Self-Confidence, Jack Welch, CEO of General Electric, discusses "bureaucracy busting" and how to set measurements that enable the organization to win.

With superb detail and humor, Arthur Carlisle investigates exactly how a very successful leader manages people, performance, and problems in "MacGregor: an Organizational Dynamics Classic Revisited." A classic can be defined as something that still works. MacGregor—the pseudonym of an oil-refinery executive—is still a classic on the 20th anniversary of its first being published.

In Leading People: Transforming Business from the Inside Out, Robert Rosen gives case studies of successful industrial leaders and condenses their various styles into what he calls the eight principles of leadership: vision, trust, participation, learning, diversity, creativity, integrity, and community. Rosen focuses on the changes that leaders have to make in their individual leadership styles in order to serve a role model for desired behavioral changes in the rest of the organization.

Robert Baugh's *Changing Work: a Union Guide to Workplace Change* builds on the experience and knowledge of its members. This AFL-CIO book is designed to be a basic tool for local union leaders to clarify and develop their mission, vision, and goals. It helps leaders set the foundation for a partnership with management and plan for educating union members about the new workplace.

Also from the AFL-CIO, *Labor Perspective on the New American Workplace: A Call for Partnership* supports union involvement in developing the new workplace and advocates active union participation in partnerships with management, beginning with planning and throughout implementation. This is the third report (previous reports were *The Changing Situation of Workers and Their Unions* and *The Future of Work*).

Trade unionists considering cooperative programs will find a practical resource in *Mutual Gains: a Guide to Union-Management Cooperation* by Cohen-Rosenthal and Burton.

A good book on the labor-management relationship is *Negotiating the Future: a Labor Perspective on American Business*. Son-and-father authors Barry and Irving Bluestone look at the subject from both sides of the table.

Michelle Kaminski and her fellow authors have done a good job with their case studies In *Making Change Happen: Six Cases of Unions and Companies Transforming Their Workplaces*.

In *Unions, Management, and Quality: Opportunities for Innovation and Excellence*, Edward Cohen-Rosenthal gives three insightful lessons: how to successfully apply quality principles to union-management change efforts, how to modify quality programs to gain enthusiastic union support, and how to overcome typical challenges associated with quality and labor relations.

Kenneth Blanchard's *One-Minute Manager* continues to be must reading for every manager. Middle managers will find Rick Maurer's *Caught in the Middle: a Leadership Guide for Partnership in the Workplace* a down-to-earth and practical resource.

In *Walk the Talk...and Get the Results You Want*, Harvey and Lucia show how good intentions can inadvertently create frustrating people problems. The authors present ways to understand what happens and ways to replace counterproductive actions with productive ones.

Joel Barker's video *Paradigm Pioneers* explores the role of leaders in bringing about new paradigms and examines why some companies are positioned to take advantage of them. Everyone is either a pioneer, exploring new territory, or a settler, hanging back until the frontier is safe. By the time it's safe, it's too late!

Joel Barker's video *Power of Vision* is truly powerful. He traveled all over the world for his examples, taken from many fields, such as Victor Frankl, the psychologist who survived Auschwitz in his determination to learn from the experience, and Eugene Lang, the philanthropist who adopted Public School 121 in Harlem school and set up scholarships and support systems that helped many youths graduate and also go on to succeed in college and beyond.

Gain Sharing is the best book on the subject. John Belcher describes and analyzes the gain sharing systems of several nationally known companies. He provides insights into the methods they use to involve employees and reward them for their contributions.

The fundamental book on the creation of the learning organization is Peter Senge's *The Fifth Discipline: the Art and Practice of the Learning Organization*. Senge looks at organizations from the systems point of view.

Performance Improvement Plan

In *The Goal*, Eliyahu Goldratt sets forth the theory of constraints: if improvements are made to any area other than constraints, or bottlenecks, the results will be suboptimal. Goldratt, an Israeli physicist, focuses on the need to make sure that activities are aligned with any organization's primary goal—to make money—and he writes his book as a novel from the viewpoint of a manufacturing plant manager. Goldratt has written a sequel, *The Race*, which elaborates on the details of these strategies. Both books are excellent.

The Haystack Syndrome: Sifting Information out of the Data Ocean is another winner from Goldratt, who always focuses on the impact of actions on the bottom line. Here he tackles the pitfalls of traditional cost accounting and how they can lead to bad decisions. He advocates ways of allocating fixed overhead that are more meaningful than the traditional methods.

R.C. Camp's *Benchmarking: the Search for Industry Best Practices that Lead to Superior Performance* is the bible on benchmarking.

Juran and Gryna's *Quality Planning and Analysis* is a basic text on the subject.

Top Management Strategy: What It Is and How to Make It Work gives an excellent basic foundation for strategic planning. Authors Tregoe and Zimmerman name nine areas of strategic importance, which they call driving forces, which help to unify what drives an organization.

Jeffrey Pfeffer tackles "When It Comes to 'Best Practices'—Why Do Smart Organizations Occasionally Do Dumb Things?" He gives solid evidence of the effectiveness of high performance, discusses barriers to implementation, and suggests how they can be overcome.

Facilitator-Key Coordinator
A highly useful pocket guide is Ralph Barra's *Tips and Techniques for Team Effectiveness*, which covers creative problem-solving, effective meetings, and interventions.

Another clear and concise reference is Goal/QPC's *The Memory Jogger: a Pocket Guide of Tools for Continuous Improvement*, which covers the seven basic tools of statistical process control.

Deployment
Theodore Levitt said it in "Marketing Myopia" two decades before the idea became a revolution. He advocated that businesses should market by meeting customer needs.

Richard Dauch's *Passion for Manufacturing* has a good section on how to team with unions and suppliers.

Edward Lawlor's *Strategic Pay* deals with aligning organizational strategies with pay systems.

Continuous Improvement Initiatives

Ralph, his incredible Normalator, Lucy, and the fire-breathing dragon are a few of the stars in *Zapp! The Lightning of Empowerment: How to Improve Quality, Productivity, and Employee Satisfaction.* Authors Byham and Cox summarize key points alongside the narrative of this corporate fable, making it easy to read either or both.

Total Quality Control by A.V. Feigenbaum is a basic text on the subject. The same is true of *Quality Control Handbook* by J.M. Juran.

In *The Wisdom of Teams: Creating the High-Performance Organization,* Katzenbach and Smith take a good, hard look at the subject and include examples of effective teams. *Inside Teams: How 20 World-Class Organizations are Winning through Teamwork* is a book of case studies of different types of teams in different environments. This book by Richard Wellins and his fellow authors works better as a reference than as a read-through.

Rummler and Brache's *Improving Performance: How to Manage White Space in the Organizational Chart* is a good how-to on process improvement, complete with examples, although that might not be obvious from the title.

James Swartz covers a number of important concepts, including paradigms, high performance, fast response, and benchmarking in *The Hunters and the Hunted: A Non-Linear Solution for American Industry.* Swartz gives many examples of turnaround companies, including Harley-Davidson, Delco Electronics, and Motorola. He recommends benchmarking companies outside one's own industry for practices to apply.

T.H. Davenport's *Process Innovation: Re-engineering Work Through Information Technology* has a heart and is better than M. Hammer's "Re-engineering Work: Don't Automate, Obliterate."

When it comes to bridging the generation gap, Morris Massey's video *What You Are Is What You Were When* is an excellent icebreaker. He helps people work better in groups because he sheds light on why people in each generation act the way they do. ("You mean you want me to come to work *every* day?") He talks so fast that few minds will have a chance to wander. He gets a lot of people laughing, but others will be turned off by his frequent use of four-letter words. *Just Get It! Massey on Values, Behavior, and Results* is an updated and diversity-ized version. The pace is slower and the content is expanded. It's socially more acceptable but less entertaining and much longer.

In *The* SMED *System* (SMED is Single Minute Exchange of Dies), Shigeo Shingo wrote the bible on quick die changes, the project that gets continuous improvement off to a good start by providing quick results. It's also available as a video.

Best Practices Report is one of the first and best reviews of practices that are proven to get results. It's by the American Quality Foundation and Ernst & Young.

Joel Barker's video *The Business of Paradigms* discusses ways to deal with paradigms, self-imposed limits that inhibit one's ability to see the benefits of new ideas. The more successful a company, the more inhibiting and restrictive are its paradigms. For example, a Swiss researcher invented the quartz crystal watch, but the Swiss, who dominated the watchmaking industry, discarded it because it had no moving parts or mainspring and thus didn't fit their definition of a watch. Texas Instruments and Seiko saw the potential of the quartz crystal, developed it, and took the market away from the Swiss. Paradigms can be identified by asking, "What today is impossible to do in our business but, if it could be done, would fundamentally change what we do?" The next step is to go beyond the boundaries. When the paradigm shifts and a new paradigm emerges, the leader loses all its advantage and goes back to square one, as the Swiss watchmakers did.

Darcy Hitchcock's *Work Redesign Team Handbook: A Step-by-Step Guide to Creating Self-Directed Teams* gives in-depth information on how to diagram leadership roles and responsibilities using the star system adapted from the Hannaford brothers' star. In *Empowered Teams: Creating Self-*

Directed Work Groups that Improve Quality, Productivity, and Participation, R.S. Wellins and fellow authors discuss the star system and much, much more.

General Strategy

James Womack and his fellow authors focuses on lean and agile manufacturing in the auto industry in America, Japan, and Europe in *The Machine That Changed the World: How Japan's Secret Weapon in the Global Auto Wars Will Revolutionize Western Industry*. Written over five years, this is MIT's $5-million study of the future of the auto industry.

In *Made in America: Regaining the Productive Edge*, Michael Dertouzos and his fellow authors focus on what organizations must do to be competitive. MIT published this book in 1989, but the concepts still apply.

Richard Schonberger has written a number of fine books. His *Japanese Manufacturing Techniques: Nine Hidden Lessons in Simplicity* covers the just-in-time strategy, also known as world-class manufacturing and lean manufacturing. His *World-Class Manufacturing: the Lessons of Simplicity Applied* is the basic text on this subject.

Out of the Crisis is a report on the quality turnaround by W.E. Deming, one of the chief gurus of quality. Kaoru Ishikawa's *What is Total Quality Control? The Japanese Way* is one of the seminal texts on the subject.

P.B. Crosby wrote two early and important texts: *Quality Is Free*, one of the books that started it all, and *Quality without Tears*.

A good and readable treatment of the basics of productivity through people is *Productive Workplaces: Organizing and Managing for Dignity, Meaning, and Community* by Marvin Weisbord.

Total Quality: An Executive's Guide for the 1990s is an excellent resource from Ernst & Young.

In *Management Practices: U.S. Companies Improve Performance through Quality Efforts*, the U.S. General Accounting Office gives a good summary, with supporting data, of the benefits of total quality management.

In *Quality or Else: The Revolution in World Business*, Dobyns and Crawford-Mason provide a general introduction and context for the high-performance workplace. A companion to the IBM-funded PBS series, this book gives a comprehensive report on the origins of the concept of quality management and discusses the changes companies will have to make to survive in the global marketplace. The authors show that, contrary to what economists have preached for years, quality costs less—not more.

BIBLIOGRAPHY

AFL-CIO Committee on the Evolution of Work. *Labor Perspective on the New American Workplace: a Call for Partnership.* Third report; publ. no. 0257-394-6.5. AFL-CIO Human Resources Development Institute. Washington, DC, 1994.

————————. *The Changing Situation of Workers and Their Unions.* Second report. 1985.

————————. *The Future of Work.* First report. 1983.

American Quality Foundation and Ernst & Young. *Best Practices Report.* American Quality Foundation, NY, 1992.

Barker, Joel. *Paradigm Pioneers.* Charthouse International Learning Center, Burnsville, MN, 1992.

————————. *The Business of Paradigms.* Charthouse International Learning Center. Burnsville, MN, 1992.

————————. *The Power of Vision.* Charthouse International Learning Center, Burnsville, MN.

Barra, Ralph. *Tips and Techniques for Team Effectiveness.* Barra International, New Oxford, PA, 1987.

Baugh, Robert. *Changing Work: A Union Guide to Workplace Change.* AFL-CIO Human Resources Development Institute, Washington, DC, 1994.

Belasco, James A., Ph.D., and Ralph A. Stayer. *Flight of the Buffalo: Soaring to Excellence, Learning to Let Employees Lead.* CorVision Media, Buffalo Grove, IL, 1994.

Belcher, John C., Jr. *Gain Sharing.* Gulf Publishing, Houston, TX, 1991.

Blanchard, Kenneth, Ph.D., and Spencer Johnson, M.D. *The One-Minute Manager: The Quickest Way to Increase Your Own Prosperity.* Berkley Publishing Group, NY, 1981.

Bluestone, Barry and Irving Bluestone. *Negotiating the Future: A Labor Perspective on American Business.* Basic Books, NY, 1992.

Brown, Mark Graham. *Baldridge Award Winning Quality: How to Interpret the Malcolm Baldridge Award Criteria.* Quality Resources, NY, 1996.

Byham, William C., Ph.D., and Jeff Cox. *Zapp! the Lightning of Empowerment: How to Improve Quality, Productivity and Employee Satisfaction.* Ballantine Books, NY, 1988.

Camp, R.C. *Benchmarking: The Search for Industry Best Practices that Lead to Superior Performance.* ASQC Quality Press, Milwaukee, WI, 1989.

Carlisle, Arthur Elliott. "MacGregor: an Organizational Dynamics Classic Revisited." *Organizational Dynamics*, American Management Assn, NY, Autumn 1995: 65-79.

Cohen-Rosenthal, Edward. *Unions, Management, and Quality: Opportunities for Innovation and Excellence.* Irwin Professional Publishing, Burr Ridge, IL, 1995.

——————————, and Cynthia E. Burton. *Mutual Gains: a Guide to Union-Management Cooperation.* ILR Press, Ithaca, NY, 1993.

Crosby, P.B. *Quality Is Free.* McGraw Hill, 1979.

——————————. *Quality without Tears.* McGraw-Hill, 1984.

Dauch, Richard E. *Passion for Manufacturing.* Society of Manufacturing Engineers, Dearborn, MI, 1993.

Davenport, T.H. *Process Innovation: Re-engineering Work through Information Technology.* Harvard Business School Press, 1993.

Deming, W.E. *Out of the Crisis.* MIT Center for Advanced Engineering Study, 1986.

Dertouzos, Michael L., Richard K. Lester, et al. *Made in America: Regaining the Productive Edge.* MIT, 1989.

Dobyns, Lloyd and Clare Crawford-Mason. *Quality or Else: the Revolution in World Business.* Houghton Mifflin, 1991.

Ernst & Young. *Total Quality: An Executive's Guide for the 1990s.* Richard D. Irwin, Homewood, IL, 1990.

Feigenbaum, A.V. *Total Quality Control*. McGraw-Hill, 1983.

Garvin, D. "How the Baldridge Award Really Works." *Harvard Business Review*, Nov-Dec 1991: 80-93.

Goal/QPC. *The Memory Jogger: A Pocket Guide of Tools for Continuous Improvement*. Goal/QPC, Methuen, MA, 1988.

Goldratt, Eliyahu M. *The Goal*. North River Press, NY, 1984.

——————————. *The Haystack Syndrome: Sifting Information out of the Data Ocean*. North River Press, NY, 1990.

——————————. *The Race*. North River Press, NY, 1986.

Hammer, M. "Re-engineering Work: Don't Automate, Obliterate." *Harvard Business Review*, Jul-Aug 1990: 104-112.

Harvey, Eric and Alexander Lucia. *Walk the Talk...and Get the Results You Want*. Treeview Publishing, Dallas, TX, 1993.

Hitchcock, Darcy. *The Work Redesign Team Handbook: A Step-by-Step Guide to Creating Self-Directed Teams*. Quality Resources, White Plains, NY, 1994.

Holtz, Lou. *If Enough People Care*. Video Publishing House, Schaumberg, IL, 1994.

Ishikawa, K. *What is Total Quality Control? The Japanese Way*. Prentice Hall, 1985.

Jones, John E., Ph.D., and J. William Pfeiffer, Ph.D., editors. *1973 Annual Handbook for Group Facilitators*. University Associates, Inc., San Diego, CA, 1973.

Juran, J.M. *Quality Control Handbook*. McGraw-Hill, 1974.

——————————— and F.M. Gryna. *Quality Planning and Analysis*. McGraw-Hill, 1993.

Kaminski, Michelle, Domenick Bertelli, et al. *Making Change Happen: Six Cases of Unions and Companies Transforming Their Workplaces*. Work and Technology Institute, Washington, DC, 1996.

Katzenbach, J.R. and Douglas K. Smith. *The Wisdom of Teams: Creating the High-Performance Organization*. Harvard Business School Press, 1993.

Lawler, Edward E., III. *Strategic Pay.* Jossey-Bass, CA, 1990.

Levitt, Theodore. "Marketing Myopia." *Harvard Business Review*, Jul-Aug 1960: 45-56.

Massey, Morris, Ph.D. *What You Are Is What You Were When.* Morris Massey Associates, Inc., Boulder, CO, 1986.

——————————. *Just Get It! Massey on Values, Behavior, and Results.* Morris Massey Associates, Boulder, CO, 1994.

Maurer, Rick. *Caught in the Middle: A Leadership Guide for Partnership in the Workplace.* Productivity Press, Cambridge, MA, 1992.

National Institute of Standards and Technology. *1996 Award Criteria: Malcolm Baldrige National Quality Award.* U.S. Department of Commerce, Washington, DC, 1996.

Pfeffer, Jeffrey. "When It Comes to 'Best Practices'—Why Do Smart Organizations Occasionally Do Dumb Things?" *Organizational Dynamics*, American Management Assn, NY, Summer 1996: 33-44.

Rosen, Robert H. *Leading People: Transforming Business from the Inside Out.* Viking Penguin, NY, 1996.

Rummler, Geary A. and Alan P. Brache. *Improving Performance: How to Manage White Space in the Organizational Chart.* Jossey-Bass, CA, 1990.

Schonberger, Richard J. *Japanese Manufacturing Techniques: Nine Hidden Lessons in Simplicity.* Free Press, NY, 1982.

——————————. *World-Class Manufacturing: The Lessons of Simplicity Applied.* Macmillan, NY, 1986.

Senge, Peter. *The Fifth Discipline: the Art and Practice of the Learning Organization.* Doubleday, NY, 1990.

Shingo, Shigeo. *The SMED System.* Productivity Press, Cambridge, MA, 1987 and (video) 1990.

Swartz, James B. *The Hunters and the Hunted: A Non-Linear Solution for American Industry.* Productivity Press, Portland, OR, 1994.

Tregoe, Benjamin B. and John W. Zimmerman. *Top Management Strategy: What It Is and How to Make It Work*. Simon & Schuster, NY, 1980.

U.S. General Accounting Office. *Management Value of High-Performance Technique Practices: U.S. Companies Improve Performance through Quality Efforts*. Washington, DC, 1991.

Weisbord, Marvin R. *Productive Workplaces: Organizing and Managing for Dignity, Meaning, and Community*. Jossey-Bass, CA, 1987.

Welch, Jack. *Speed, Simplicity, and Self-Confidence*. Video Publishing House, Schaumberg, IL, 1993.

Wellins, Richard S., William C. Byham, and George R. Pixon. *Inside Teams: How 20 World-Class Organizations Are Winning through Teamwork*. Jossey-Bass, CA, 1994.

——————————, and J.M. Wilson. *Empowered Teams: Creating Self-Directed Work Groups that Improve Quality, Productivity, and Participation*. Jossey-Bass, San Francisco, CA, 1991.

Womack, James P., Daniel T. Jones, and Daniel Roos. *The Machine That Changed the World: How Japan's Secret Weapon in the Global Auto Wars Will Revolutionize Western Industry*. Macmillan, NY, 1990.

INDEX

A

action plan 39, 90, 94
Alternate Dispute Resolution 71.
  (**See also** Win-Win)
analysis chart 91
appraisal 29, 60, 63-65, 75-77,
  85-88, 96, 107, 140, 141

assessment 3, 5, 10, 11, 16,
  24, 29, 39, 57, 146, 153,
  190, 198, 201

B

balanced scorecard 11, 12
Baldridge core values and concepts 12

brainstorming 89, 91, 99
business results 14, 133

C

cascading approach 196
cause-and-effect diagram 90.
  (**See also** Fishbone)
communication 6, 9, 10, 15, 17-20,
  26, 27, 32, 34, 44, 46, 52, 60,
  70, 73, 77, 81, 116-121, 125,
  129, 132, 146, 147, 193,
  197-199
conflict resolution 24, 36, 67, 71-72
consensus 24, 36, 63, 71, 73, 89-92,
  99, 115, 126, 128, 174, 177, 196, 197
continuous improvement 4, 12,
  14, 18, 23, 29, 51, 57, 61,62,
  64, 65, 76-78, 83-85, 88,96,
  102, 103, 105, 107, 140, 169,
  171, 173, 184, 186, 189, 190,
  192-194, 204, 207
convergent thinking 88, 89, 99

cooperation 6, 14, 15, 17-21, 62
  77, 99, 112, 129, 156, 258, 202
corporate responsibility 12
cost of quality 51-56, 59, 64, 86, 184
cultural criteria 14
culture 4-6, 10, 26, 34, 42, 48,50,
  58-60, 62, 98, 102, 130-134,
  136, 138, 140, 143, 144, 147, 151
  160, 164, 166, 182-186, 191, 195
customer focus 13, 14, 80, 111
  140
customer satisfaction 1, 3,
  12-14, 27, 40-42, 49, 51, 53,
  54, 59, 97, 103, 104, 121,
  123, 125, 131, 146-148, 170,
  186, 188, 193
customer-driven quality 12
cycle time 12, 51-53, 59, 64, 94-97

I

J

K

L

M

Malcolm Baldridge National
  Quality Award 11, 57,
  140, 141, 153, 186, 201
management by fact 12, 186
managers 15, 18, 19, 23, 24, 31,
  34, 42, 48-50, 52, 59, 61, 62, 77,
  88, 98, 104-107, 112, 114, 118,
  132, 133, 137, 138, 140, 145,

  148, 152, 153, 184, 194, 203
manufacturing cost 54, 78
measurement 5, 10, 11, 30,
  39-41, 46, 48, 51-53, 64,
  76, 94, 118, 133, 138, 139
  188, 201
modern operating agreement
  19, 109, 113, 118

O

openness 35

P

paradigms 25, 70, 89, 145,
  203-206
Pareto principle 91
partnerships, customer-supplier
  75, 77, 78, 82
pay for knowledge 29
pay for performance 29
performance appraisal 63, 64,
  75-77
positive operational and financial
results 14
prevention 12, 51, 54, 55, 86,
  178, 183, 185, 186, 189

problem-solving 24, 36, 42, 53,
  62, 80, 83, 88-90, 92, 96, 100,
  104, 105, 118, 123-125, 130,
  135, 137, 149, 184, 193, 198,
  204
process cycle time 53, 56
process management 14, 135,
  139
process mapping 110
profit sharing 29, 30, 126, 197
pyramid of measurements 40

Q

QS 9000 11, 83-85, 87, 128, 167,

quality audit 54, 80

R

S

T

V

W

THE AUTHORS

Timothy J. Herron is vice president of WINOC. He has 25 years of manufacturing management experience in labor relations and operations in positions ranging from first-line supervisor to plant manager. For the past 15 years, he has served as a consultant on the design and implementation of people-based performance improvement systems. He has coached, trained, and facilitated groups of direct labor, middle managers, presidents, CEOs, and union leaders in many organizations including: Allen Bradley, B.F. Goodrich, Centerior Energy, ITT Automotive, LTV Steel, MTD, Oglebay Norton, The Ohio Manufacturers' Association, University Hospitals, and Zircoa. Tim has completed two study missions to Japan analyzing the role of employee involvement in performance improvement in the steel and automotive industries.

George P. Bohan is manager of advisory services for WINOC. He has more than 20 years of experience in mining, manufacturing, service, health care, and the public sector. George specializes in all phases of implementing high-performance work systems from design, assessment and leadership development to training and facilitating teams. He has been an advisor to many organizations including: Avery Dennison, Eaton Corp., the City of Lakewood, Lamson and Sessions, LTV Steel, Mt.Sinai Medical Center, Republic Engineered Steels, and Stouffers Hotels and Resorts. He has presented to local and national audiences and has been published in journals and business publications on the systems required to support the successful implementation of high-performance concepts.

Robert P. Meyer is president of WINOC and has been with the organization since its founding in 1981. He has served as an examiner for the Malcolm Baldrige National Quality Award and has more than 25 years of industrial experience. He has helped a variety of organizations understand the benefits of people-based approaches to quality and productivity improvement. Bob is a charter member of the Human Resources Division of the American Society of Quality Control and a past president of the Cleveland Chapter of the Association of Quality and Participation. He serves on the boards of the Inter-American Network of Quality and Productivity Centers and the National Labor Management Association.

Work In Northeast Ohio Council
6200 Rockside Woods Blvd, Suite 300
Independence, Ohio 44131
      phone: (216) 520-0770
      fax: (216) 520-0776
      e-mail: winocs@aol.com